GCSE RE For You

Christianity

Anne Jordan

Stanley Thornes (Publishers) Ltd

Printed and bound in China by Dah Hua Printing Press Co. Ltd.
Page make-up by Pentacor PLC, High Wycombe
Illustrated by Jane Taylor and Steve Ballinger
Picture research by Christina Morgan

First published in 2000 by:
Stanley Thornes (Publishers) Ltd
Ellenborough House
Wellington Street
CHELTENHAM GL50 1YW
England

00 01 02 03 04 / 10 9 8 7 6 5 4 3 2 1

A catalogue record for this book is available from the British Library.

ISBN 0-7487-5320-6

Acknowledgements
With thanks to the following for permission to reproduce photographs and other
copyright material in this book:

Andes Press Agency/Carlos Reyes Manzo 8, 11 (top), 26, 28 (top), 29, 35, 36, 38, 57
(centre), 62, 64, 71, 80, 84, 87, 89, 96, 99 (top and bottom), 105 (bottom), 108
(bottom), 109; BBC Photo Library 11 (bottom); Bridgeman Art Library:
Louvre/Giraudon 55, *Santa Maria della Grazie, Italy* 47; Circa Photo Library: 51, 90,
Mike Edwards 28 (bottom), 104 (bottom), *Bipinchandra J. Mistry* 108 (top), *Ged
Murray* 68, 95 (bottom), *John Smith* 104 (top); Hutchison: *Mischa Scorer* 59, *Andrey
Zvoznikov* 83; By kind permission of the Salvation Army: 97 (top) *Robin Bryant* 88,
Stomebrink 99 (centre); Jerry Wooldridge 57 (top).

Every effort has been made to contact copyright holders. The publishers apologise to
anyone whose rights have been inadvertently overlooked, and will be happy to rectify
any errors or omissions.

Contents

Topic 1

Who was Jesus?

An early painting of Jesus

What is ...?

Christianity is the faith tradition in which the followers believe that Jesus of Nazareth is the Son of God. Christians call Jesus, 'Christ'.

Christ is the Greek word for the 'chosen' or 'anointed' one of God. It is equivalent to the Hebrew word 'Messiah'. Christians believe that Jesus was chosen by God to bring about His kingdom on earth and to lead people back to God.

Jesus was a Jew, born between 6 BCE and 4 BCE in Palestine (the country now called Israel). His mother was Mary and her husband was a carpenter called Joseph. It is thought that Jesus followed this trade until he was about 30 years old. Although Jesus was brought up in the town of Nazareth in Galilee, he is thought to have been born in Bethlehem, in Judaea. Before he began his ministry, Jesus was baptised in the River Jordan by his cousin, John the Baptist. Jesus began to travel around the Sea of Galilee, where he preached to the people, and gathered followers. Miracles became associated with him and his followers accepted him as God's chosen leader. After he had preached for about three years, Jesus was executed on a cross outside the city of Jerusalem. Christians do not think that this was the end of the story and believe that three days later Jesus rose from the dead. His followers saw Jesus over the next 40 days. Christians believe Jesus returned to heaven, where he still lives and watches over the world, and from where he will return to earth at the end of time.

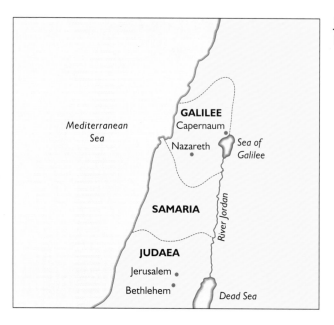

Jesus was born in Palestine in about 6 BCE

The Early Church

The followers of Jesus began to spread the Christian message throughout the Roman Empire. One of the early converts to Christianity was Saul of Tarsus. After he became a Christian, Saul became known as Paul. He travelled around the Mediterranean, preaching the Christian message and establishing Christian churches. He wrote letters to these churches to guide them in the Christian faith. Many of these letters survive in the part of the Bible called the New Testament. It is thought that the Emperor Nero put Paul to death in Rome, in 64 CE.

The Early Church had shared beliefs about Jesus and worshipped in the same way. It was one united church. Christian groups would meet together to read the scriptures, listen to a talk about the Christian faith, to pray and to praise God. This usually took place early on Sunday morning. A leader called either an elder or a bishop led each local group of Christians. The most important bishop was the bishop of Rome, because Jesus' disciple, Peter, was believed to have been the first bishop of Rome. As time passed, Christians began to disagree as to who should lead the groups, the form the worship should take and how Christian beliefs should be understood. This led to splits within the Christian Church.

 What do you think?

Why do you think splits were caused in the Early Christian Church?

 Questions

1 Write a brief biography of Jesus.
2 a Who was Saul of Tarsus?
  b Why is Saul important to Christians?
3 Describe and explain the way in which early Christians worshipped.

Activity

1 Draw the map of Palestine in your book.
2 Mark on the map the following places: Bethlehem, Nazareth, Jerusalem, the River Jordan and the Sea of Galilee.
3 Underneath the map, list the places you have marked. Explain how each place is linked to the life of Jesus.

What is …?

The Church is the term used to describe the world-wide body of Christians.

A church is used to describe either a group of Christians worshipping together, or the building in which they worship.

The Christian Church divides

What is…?

A **schism** is a division of a group into opposing groups.

Activity

Look at page 14 to find out what Christians understand by the Trinity.

The Great Schism

The first major division in Christianity took place in 1054 CE between the Orthodox and Roman Catholic churches. This event is known as the Great Schism. The two areas of disagreement that caused the division were:

- Who should be leader of the Christian Church. Christians in the West believed that it should be the Bishop of Rome, the Pope, because he was the successor to St Peter. The Christians in the East did not agree. They could not accept that only one person could have the authority to decide church matters.
- The way in which the Trinity was to be understood.

The Orthodox Church

Orthodox Christians believe that their Church has preserved the tradition and continuity of the faith established by Jesus. The Church calls itself 'orthodox' because it has continued the 'right' or 'orthodox' way of belief and worship. The Church does not have one overall leader, but several leaders called **patriarchs**.

The Roman Catholic Church

The Pope is head of the Roman Catholic Church and is based in Rome. Roman Catholics accepted the Pope as the successor to St Peter, the first Bishop of Rome, who was given his authority to lead the Church by Jesus himself, and therefore the authority of the Pope comes directly from God. Catholic means 'universal', and the Roman Catholic Church believes that it has the right way of worship for all Christians, world-wide.

The Reformation

A further split in the Christian Church took place in the sixteenth century. Some Christians became dissatisfied with the way in which the Roman Catholic Church was organised, and began to protest about the teachings and practices of the Catholic Church. These Christians wanted reform and they became known as **Protestants**. The Protestants began to set up different ways of worship and many different Protestant groups were formed, and continue to be formed today. Some of the best-known branches of the Protestant Church are the Baptists, Methodists, the Pentecostal Church, the Society of Friends, or Quakers, and the Salvation Army.

The Church of England

The Church of England is also called the **Anglican Church**. It is a Protestant Church, but in many ways, it has kept the Catholic tradition in its beliefs, practices and styles of worship. The Church of England split away from Rome in 1539 CE because Henry VIII wanted a divorce from his wife, Catherine of Aragon. The Pope would not grant the divorce so Henry made himself Head of the Church in England and granted himself a divorce. Henry was not against the Roman Catholic form of worship and therefore retained many of its features. The monarch is still the Supreme Governor of the Church of England and the main leader of the Church is the Archbishop of Canterbury. The Church of England is the established Church in England. Any other Protestant churches in England are called Nonconformist or Free churches.

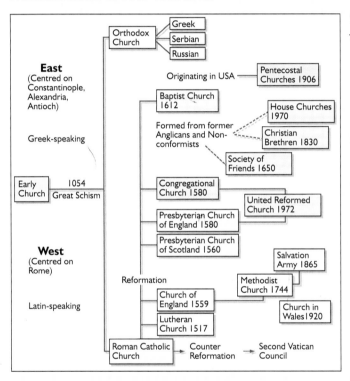

Denominations within the Christian Church

A **denomination** is a church or religious group.

A **Free Church** is a Protestant denomination free from the control of the Church of England.

A **Nonconformist** Church is a Protestant denomination that does not conform to the beliefs and worship of the Church of England.

1 Choose **one** Christian denomination from the chart.
2 Find out how it came to be formed.
3 Write a brief history of this denomination in your book.

The Ecumenical Movement

Many Christians think that it is wrong that Christianity is split into so many different churches. The Ecumenical Movement tries to bring churches back together. The word 'ecumenical' means 'one world'.

? Questions

1 What was the Great Schism?
2 Why does the Orthodox Church believe it is 'orthodox'?
3 Explain how the Roman Catholic Church got its name.
4 What was the Reformation?
5 Explain how the Church of England is different from other Protestant churches.
6 What is the Ecumenical Movement trying to achieve?
7 'It does not matter how you worship so long as you worship.' Do you think all Christians would agree? Give reasons for your answer, showing that you have thought about more than one point of view.

Topic 3

Leaders of the Christian churches

What is ...?

Ordination is the ceremony at which a Christian denomination admits someone into the priesthood or ministry.

Christians believe God has called people to be leaders in their church, and that to be a leader is a **vocation**. Christians do not agree on the role of the leader in the services.

In the Church of England, Roman Catholic and Orthodox churches, it is believed that the ordained person becomes the link between God and the people. Other churches believe that everyone is equal before God, and that the leader is no different from the congregation. The leader is there to guide and to minister to the people.

Priests

The leaders in the Church of England, Roman Catholic and Orthodox churches are called priests. These churches believe that, because the ordained priest has a special relationship with God, the priest is able to consecrate (ie to dedicate to God) the bread and wine during the service of Holy Communion, to hear confession and offer absolution as well as administering the other sacraments. A priest is usually in charge of a **parish**. Senior priests are called **bishops**. They are in charge of a **diocese**, which is made up of several parishes. Senior bishops are called **archbishops**.

The priest wears vestments because:

What is ...?

Confession is the time when Christians say sorry to God for the sins they have committed.

Absolution is the forgiveness given by the priest for the sins confessed to the priest if the priest believes the person is truly sorry for their sins.

Sacrament is the name given to a service at which there is an outward sign of an inner gift from God. It is a service at which Christians believe they come closer to God.

- the authority of the priests is believed to come in a direct line from Jesus, through the Apostles, and each generation of bishops. This is called **Apostolic Succession**. The vestments are based on the clothes worn by the leaders of the Early Church and therefore symbolise this unbroken link from the time of Christ;
- the vestments show that the leader of the service has a special role and relationship with God;
- the individual items worn show whether the person is a deacon, priest or bishop. A bishop in the Roman Catholic Church and the Church of England wears a special hat called a **mitre** and carries a shepherd's crook called a **crozier**. The mitre represents the tongues of fire that came at Pentecost. The crozier, because it is a shepherd's crook, shows that the bishop is like a shepherd protecting his flock.

The priest will wear special robes called **vestments**

A bishop wears a mitre and carries a crozier

Activity

1 Read the account of the first Pentecost on page 53.
2 Explain the link between the shape of the bishop's mitre and the events of Pentecost.

Ministers

The Free churches believe that everyone is equal before God, and therefore the leader usually wears ordinary clothes to take the services. The leader is trained to help the people to understand the Christian message and how to live as God would wish. The leader is often called minister or pastor because of this role as guide or helper.

The role of a priest or minister
Although there may be different views about the authority of the leader of the Christian denomination, the role of a priest or minister is very similar. The role includes:

- leading the services, including preaching the Word of God
- performing baptisms, marriages and funeral services
- guiding the congregation to a better understanding of the Christian message
- visiting the sick and dying
- organising charity work.

Some Christian denominations do not have priests or ministers. For example, the Society of Friends (Quakers) believe that when an individual feels moved to speak in an act of worship, he or she is ministering to others in the group.

Questions

1 a Explain the terms 'vocation' and 'ordination'.
   b How are these two terms linked?
2 Explain the differences between a priest and a minister.
3 What tasks would priests and ministers consider important?
4 'The leader of a Christian denomination must never break the law.'
   Do you agree? Give reasons for your answer, showing that you have thought about more than one point of view.

Do you understand...
Christianity

Task 1

1 What do you think were the **three** most important events in the life of Jesus?
2 The followers of Jesus believed that he rose from the dead after his crucifixion. Do you think that Christianity would have become a world-wide faith if this event had not happened? Give reasons for your answer, showing that you have thought about more than one point of view.

Task 2

The extract below is taken from St Paul's letter to the people of Corinth (1 Corinthians 13: 1–8)

If I speak in the tongues of men and of angels, but have not love, I am only a resounding gong or a clanging cymbal. If I have the gift of prophecy and can fathom all mysteries and all knowledge, and if I have a faith that can move mountains, but have not love, I am nothing. If I give all I possess to the poor and surrender my body to the flames, but have not love, I gain nothing. Love is patient, love is kind. It does not envy, it does not boast, it is not proud. It is not rude, it is not self-seeking, it is not easily angered, it keeps no record of wrongs. Love does not delight in evil but rejoices with the truth. It always protects, always trusts, always hopes, always perseveres. Love never fails.

1 Explain why St Paul wrote letters to the early Christian churches.
2 a Explain the values a Christian is expected to have according to St Paul's letter to the people of Corinth.
   b How would you expect these values to influence the way in which Christians live their lives and the way in which they treat other people?
3 'Nobody can really follow the example of Jesus.' Do you think that Christians would agree? Give reasons for your answer, showing that you have thought about more than one point of view.

Task 3

1 What are the **three** major divisions in Christianity?
2 Explain what caused each of these divisions in the Christian Church.
3 'Splits in Christianity are not what Jesus wants.' Do you agree? Give reasons for your answer, showing that you have thought about more than one point of view.

Task 4

Members of the Salvation Army wear uniforms and have the same ranks as soldiers. An officer such as a Captain will take the services. The head of the Salvation Army is called the General. Members of the Salvation Army believe that they are a well-trained, disciplined army fighting for God's cause. This means that besides attending acts of worship, members of the denomination work with people with problems, such as alcoholics, drug addicts and the homeless.

Members of the Salvation Army wear a uniform

1 Why do you think that the members of the Salvation Army believe that they are fighting in God's cause?
2 Members of the Salvation Army spend a lot of time working with people with problems. Explain why they feel that this is an important part of the life of a Christian.
3 'It does not matter what the person leading a service wears.' Do you agree? Give reasons for your answer, showing that you have thought about more than one point of view.

Task 5

1 Explain why many Christians believe that it is important to have an ordained person to lead them in worship.
2 What other tasks would you expect a priest or minister to undertake?
3 'A priest or minister must believe in God.' Do you agree? Give reasons for your opinion, showing that you have thought about more than one point of view.

Dawn French as the Vicar of Dibley

Task 6

The Roman Catholic and Orthodox churches do not ordain women. There are several reasons for this, including the view that as Jesus did not include a woman as one of the twelve Apostles then it is wrong for Christian leaders to be women, and the fact that St Paul said that women must be silent in church.

The Church of England has accepted that Jesus and St Paul lived at a time when women did not take a public role but as times have changed then women should be allowed to enter the priesthood.

'Women should be allowed to be ordained as leaders of their church.' Do you agree? Give reasons for your answer, showing that you have thought about more than one point of view.

Topic 1 Creeds

 **What is ...?**

A creed is a statement of religious beliefs agreed by a faith to be true. The word 'creed' comes from the Latin word 'credo', which means 'I believe'. There are two main creeds used in the Christian church. These are the Apostles' Creed and the Nicene Creed.

Creeds are often stated during services to remind Christians:

- of their main beliefs
- what it means to be a Christian
- as a public statement of what Christians have in common
- to show how Christianity is different from other faiths.

 Activity

Write out the Apostles' Creed in your book and learn it.

The Apostles' Creed is one of the statements of the beliefs shared by Christians. The creed gets its name because it preserves the beliefs of the first followers of Jesus.

The Apostles' Creed

I believe in God the Father, Almighty, the Creator of heaven and earth,
And in Jesus Christ, His only son, our Lord.
Who was conceived of the Holy Spirit,
Born of the Virgin Mary,
Suffered under Pontius Pilate, was crucified, dead and buried;
He descended into hell.
The third day he rose again from the dead;
He ascended into heaven, and sits at the right-hand of God the Father Almighty.
Whence He shall come to judge the living and the dead.
I believe in the Holy Spirit,
the holy catholic church,
the communion of saints,
the forgiveness of sins,
the resurrection of the body,
and the life everlasting.
Amen.

 What do you think?

'God does not exist because there is so much suffering in the world.'
Write a speech for or against this statement for a class debate.

'God the Father, Almighty, the Creator of heaven and earth'

The opening statement of the Apostles' Creed explains what Christians believe about God the Father. Christians believe:

- God exists
- there is only one God
- God loves them like a 'father' loves his children
- God is perfect
- God is omnipotent (all-powerful), the '**Almighty**'
- God is beyond human understanding
- God is the '**creator of heaven and earth**', and every creature within heaven and earth. God made everything and therefore everything belongs to God
- God is in three parts; God the Father, God the Son and God the Holy Spirit.

God the Father

Christians believe God has revealed himself as the perfect '**Father**'. A father loves and cares for his children, and he wants the best for them but must allow them the freedom to make mistakes and hopefully grow as a result. As a good father, God guides and disciplines his children. God will judge his 'children' on how they have lived by his rules. Christians believe it is their duty to please God by living by his rules and avoiding sin.

Christians believe God the Father is **Almighty** because there is no other being with God's power. Christians believe:

- there is nothing that God cannot do
- God is in control of everything (**omnipotent**).
- God is everywhere at once (**omnipresent**). This means that God knows everything past, present and future
- God sustains and rules everything.

What is...?

Christians believe that the **Trinity** is the name given to the three combined parts of God.

The three parts of the one God are God the Father; God the Son; and God the Holy Spirit. These three forms or aspects are separate but at the same time still God. It is rather like the way water can be a solid (ice), a liquid (water) or a gas (steam), and still be water.

St Patrick used the shamrock to explain the Trinity

 **What is...?**

People who believe in God use the word **sin**, to mean an action which goes against God's laws, or which separates people from God.

Questions

1 What is a creed?
2 Why do Christians use creeds during their services?
3 What do Christians mean when they speak of the Trinity?
4 'God, the Father, Almighty, the Creator of heaven and earth.' Explain what Christians mean when they say these words from the Apostles' Creed.

Topic 2

The Trinity

Activity

Look back to page 4. Who was Jesus?

What is ...?

The Fall of Man is the name given to the story in Genesis of the disobedience of Adam and Eve in the Garden of Eden. Christians believe that when Adam chose to disobey God, he introduced sin into the world. This first sin is called 'original sin', and it is inherited by all humans. Christians believe that humans have to avoid this inherited temptation to sin.

Christians believe that the Trinity is the three combined parts of God: God the Father, God the Son and God the Holy Spirit (see page 13).

God the Son

Christians believe God the Son is Jesus.

When Christians say that they believe '**in Jesus Christ, his only Son, our Lord**', they are stating that they believe that:

- Jesus is their **saviour**. The name Jesus means 'God saves'. Adam's disobedience separated God and humans. Christians believe Jesus suffered and died to gain God's forgiveness and to open the way back to God.
- Jesus is God's **only Son**. Jesus' relationship with God the Father is different to the relationship God has with any other creature, because Jesus is God in human form. Christians believe that Jesus is both truly human and truly divine. Jesus can only be a perfect sacrifice to gain God's forgiveness because he is both God and man.
- Christians call Jesus '**Lord**' because Jesus is to be obeyed. He is the master who must be worshipped. Christians serve Jesus by being obedient to his teaching throughout their lives.
- Jesus is the **Christ**. Christians believe Jesus had been chosen by God to lead people back to God and to bring about the Kingdom of God on earth.

What is ...?

Incarnation means 'taking on flesh'. Christians use incarnation to describe their belief that God came down to earth in the human form of Jesus.

Activity

Look at page 4. What do the words 'Christ' and 'Messiah' mean?

'**Who was conceived of the Holy Spirit, Born of the Virgin Mary**'
According to the Apostles' Creed, Jesus '**was conceived of the Holy Spirit**' and '**born of the Virgin Mary**'. Christians believe that:

- Jesus is a human name. They believe that Jesus lived on earth as a human, but was also **divine**, because Jesus was God in human form, (**incarnate**).
- Jesus was '**conceived of the Holy Spirit**', so his birth was unique. This is evidence to Christians that Jesus is God's Son.
- Jesus did not inherit original sin because he was 'conceived by the Holy Spirit' and 'born of the Virgin Mary'. Christians accept that Jesus was 'born of the Virgin Mary', but do not agree what this means.

The **Roman Catholic** and **Orthodox churches** teach that Mary was born without sin. This was important so that Jesus would not inherit the sinful nature passed on to each generation since the Fall. Mary remained a virgin all her life. Mary is given a high place in these churches, and prayers are said to her, to ask her to **intercede** (speak up) for the individual to God. Both churches believe that Mary's body was taken up to heaven when she died. This event is called the **Assumption**.

Protestants do not agree. Many Protestants believe that Mary was a virgin when Jesus was born, but after his birth, she lived a normal life as wife and mother. Some Protestants **do not believe** that **Mary was a virgin** when Jesus was born. They believe that she was a young woman who conceived Jesus in the normal way. The Holy Spirit entered the baby when he was born, and this is how Jesus became the Son of God.

Christians believe that the Virgin Mary was the mother of Jesus

What do you think?

In Mark's Gospel, on one occasion, Jesus is told that 'your mother, brothers and sisters are outside, and they want you'.

How do you think that the churches which believe Mary remained a virgin all her life explain this reference in Mark's Gospel?

How do you think other Christians might interpret the passage?

Questions

1 What does the Apostles' Creed teach about the birth of Jesus?
2 What event do Christians remember when they refer to the Fall of Man?
3 What does 'incarnation' mean?
4 Why is it important to many Christians that Mary was a virgin when Jesus was born?
5 'It is not possible to be a Christian and not to believe in the Virgin Birth.' Do you agree? Give reasons for your answer, showing that you have thought about more than one point of view.

'Suffered under Pontius Pilate, was crucified, dead and buried'.
Christians believe that it was on **Good Friday** that:

- Jesus '**suffered under Pontius Pilate**' when the Roman governor, Pontius Pilate, ordered that Jesus was to be whipped and nailed to a cross
- Jesus died on the cross. This event is called the **Crucifixion**
- after death, Jesus' body was removed from the cross and buried in the tomb of Joseph of Arimathea. The tomb was sealed with a stone and Roman soldiers were placed on guard.

What is ...?

Christians, Jews and Muslims believe that **hell** is the place where some people who have committed sins are sent. There are different understandings of what hell is like, but the three faiths all agree that it means to be separated from God.

'He descended into hell'
This refers to Jesus going down to hell to free sinners. The reason for Jesus' death was to open the way back to God. Christians believe that only Jesus could bring them back to God, because:

i) Jesus as God was the perfect sacrifice;
ii) Jesus as man could represent people when he offered his life in exchange for forgiveness for the sins of the world. The price he paid to redeem people was his suffering and death on the cross. This freed Christians from the everlasting spiritual death of exile from God. This is known as the **Atonement**.

Christians remember this event on **Holy Saturday**, the name given to the day between Good Friday and Easter Sunday.

'On the third day he rose again'
Early on Sunday morning the women returned to the tomb and found it empty. Christians believe Jesus had risen from the dead, and call the event the **Resurrection**. It is the central belief of Christianity that Jesus rose again. Christians celebrate the event every Sunday, but particularly on Easter Sunday.

The resurrection of Jesus is important to Christians because Christians believe it proves that:

- Jesus was the Son of God
- through his suffering on the cross, Jesus had conquered sin and death, and opened the way back to God
- Jesus had proved that God was willing to forgive people who obey his wishes
- Jesus had shown that death was not the end. There is life after death
- it is possible for people who follow Jesus to be forgiven for their sins and to be with God after death
- Jesus is the **Redeemer**. Mankind needed to be saved from sin (**redeemed**) because breaking God's laws (sinning) leads to separation from God.

The resurrection of Jesus is the most important event for Christians. St Paul said, 'If Christ has not been raised from death, then we have nothing to preach... if Christ has not been raised, then your faith is a delusion and you are still lost to your sins.'

What do you think St Paul meant by these words?

Activity

Imagine you are a Christian who wants to encourage people to attend their local church. Design a leaflet to be sent to each house in the neighbourhood explaining why people should attend the church.

Christians argue about the facts and meaning of the Resurrection. Was it a **spiritual** or a **bodily** resurrection? Some Christians believe it was **only the spirit** of Jesus that was resurrected. The majority of Christians believe that Jesus was resurrected in his bodily form.

Fundamentalist Christians believe everything happened as stated in the Gospels.

Roman Catholics and **Orthodox Christians** believe that Jesus was altered at the resurrection into a new, immortal human form.

Some **Liberal Christians** believe that only the spirit of Jesus rose and his body remained in the tomb.

Questions

1 He 'suffered under Pontius Pilate, was crucified, dead and buried.' Explain what Christians mean when they say these words from the Apostles' Creed.
2 'He descended into hell.' Explain what Christians mean when they say these words from the Apostles' Creed.
3 Why does the Creed emphasise the importance of the crucifixion and resurrection of Jesus?
4 Why do you think that the cross has become one of the greatest symbols of Christianity?
5 Explain the different ways in which Christians understand the phrase 'on the third day he rose again'.
6 Do you think that it matters how Christians understand the line in the creed, 'on the third day he rose again'? Give reasons for your answer, and show that you have thought about more than one point of view.

'He ascended into heaven and sits at the right-hand of God the Father Almighty.'

Christians agree that Jesus rose from the dead and is still alive in heaven. He completed his work on earth and was carried up to heaven (**ascended**) 40 days after his resurrection. Jesus told his followers that he would be in heaven until the end of time. He would be with them although they would be unable to see him. Christians remember this event on **Ascension Day**.

Christians believe Jesus sits in the honoured position next to God in heaven. The position at the '**right-hand of God**' is showing Jesus' importance, as this is a place of honour, the place occupied by the heir or the most trusted counsellor of a ruler. The idea is to show the importance of the part played by Jesus in saving humanity.

Christians believe Jesus' ascension means:

- Jesus is accessible to all. Only by returning to heaven could Jesus be everywhere at once. This means that Jesus is able to fulfil his promise to be with everyone until the end of time.
- By returning to heaven, Jesus was able to send the power of the Holy Spirit to guide people.
- Jesus said that he needed to go to prepare a place in heaven for people. This means by returning to heaven Jesus is making it possible for those who follow him to go to heaven.
- As it is not possible to see Jesus then Christians have to have true faith in his existence.

 **What do you think?**

The disciple Thomas would not believe that Jesus had risen from the dead until he saw him for himself. Jesus told Thomas, 'Because you have seen me, you have believed; blessed are those who have not seen and yet have believed' (John 20: 29). What do you think Jesus meant by 'Blessed are those who have not seen and yet have believed'?

'Whence He shall come to judge the living and the dead'

There is no general agreement among Christians about when and how Jesus will return. The events surrounding Jesus' return are called the **Day of Judgement**. Most Christians believe the Day of Judgement will occur at the end of time, at a time known only to God. It is from his position at the right-hand of God that Jesus will return to judge everyone, both those who are alive at the time and those who have already died. He will decide their eternal fate in either heaven or hell, according to the way they have followed his example and lived by God's rules. Christians believe that at the end of time God's kingdom will be established on earth.

Christians accept that God will base his judgement of them by the way in which they have:

- loved and served God
- used their special gifts from God
- shown love for others.

Christians believe Jesus will return at the end of time

God the Holy Spirit

Christians accept that the third part of the Trinity is God the Holy Spirit, and that the Holy Spirit is:

- the part of God that works within the world
- the power of God which brings spiritual life and understanding of God
- the invisible power of God which breathes new life into people. 'Spirit' means 'wind' or 'breath'
- the part of God that changes people into the sort of person God wants
- the help and guidance from God to help people to make the right choices and decisions so that they will lead better lives and overcome the temptation to do wrong
- an aid to prayer.

? Questions

1 In what ways would you expect a belief in the Holy Spirit to influence an individual Christian's life?

2 Explain what Christians mean when they say the following words from the Apostles' Creed:
i) 'ascended into heaven';
ii) 'sits at the right-hand of the Father';
iii) 'whence he shall come to judge both the living and the dead'.

Topic 3

Christian beliefs about the Church

Activity

Using the following information, write a detailed description in your book of the Christian understanding of the Church as stated in the Creed.

The final section of the Apostles' Creed is a summary of the major beliefs of Christians about the Christian church.

'The holy catholic church'

'Holy' means 'set apart for God, or by God'. The Church is the sacred representation of God's will on earth. It provides the physical presence of Christ and continues his work in the world. It is '**catholic**' because it is the **universal** community of Christians as established by Jesus.

'The communion of saints'

Christians believe **all Christians**, living and dead, are parts of one family in Christ. They are in **communion** with each other regardless of race, colour or class. Death does not end this fellowship. When Christians pray they must be aware of the Christians who have lived before. The use of the word '**saints**' in the creed means **all** followers of Jesus, both living and dead. Some Christians believe that the 'saints' are limited to one kind of Christian, those 'born again' or converted, whereas other Christians believe that they include all Christian movements and groups.

The phrase, '**the communion of saints**' is saying that those who accept Jesus Christ as God's only son and their Lord join in fellowship or partnership with all people who have accepted the Christian faith. This fellowship is not limited by time and includes those Christians who have already died and those Christians not yet born.

What do you think?

Why do you think that Christians believe it is important to be aware of other Christians both living and dead?

'The forgiveness of sins'

Christians believe that when people commit sins the personal bond with God is broken. Only God can **forgive** sin. God has shown that he is willing to forgive sinners by sending his son, Jesus. To be forgiven, sinners must realise that they have done wrong, turn back to God and ask God's forgiveness. God's forgiveness will only be given to those who have turned back to God, are truly sorry and show forgiveness to others. Christians believe membership of the Christian Church helps to strengthen an individual's ability to overcome the temptation to do wrong.

'The resurrection of the body and life everlasting'

Christians believe that death is only the continuation of an eternal life with God for those who have accepted Christ. Christians accept this eternal life begins when a person accepts the Christian faith. This is why baptism for many Christians is seen as 'rebirth', because it is the beginning of an individual's life in the Christian faith. This means that Christians believe that when they die, there will be the **'resurrection of the body'**, and **'life everlasting'** with God.

Christians disagree about the form the 'resurrection of the body' will take.

Orthodox and **Roman Catholic Christians** believe that the whole body is resurrected in a new immortal form. Many Christians believe in a **spiritual resurrection**; the **soul** leaves the body and goes on to an eternal life.

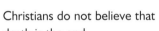

What is ...?

Eternal means existing always without a beginning or end in time.
Immortal means to live for ever.

Christians do not believe that death is the end

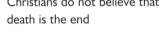

What do you think?

'I do not mind what form I take after death so long as there is life after death.'

Do you agree or disagree with this statement? Give reasons for your view.

Questions

1 Explain the meaning then state any differences of understanding amongst Christians of the following phrases:
   i) 'the holy catholic church'
   ii) 'the forgiveness of sins'
   iii) 'the communion of saints'
   iv) 'the resurrection of the body and the life everlasting'.
2 Explain how the Resurrection of Jesus is linked to the Christian belief that Christians can achieve 'the resurrection of the body and the life everlasting'.

Do you understand...

Christian beliefs?

Task 1

1 Draw a diagram to explain the Christian understanding of the Trinity.
2 Explain the **three** parts of God as stated in the Apostles' Creed.
3 God the Holy Spirit is often represented as a dove. Why do you think that this symbol was chosen to represent the Holy Spirit? (Read the account of the baptism of Jesus on page 42 to help you answer the question.)

Task 2

The following parable is a description of the Day of Judgement and how Jesus will judge people on that day.

The Parable of the Sheep and the Goats (Matthew 25: 31–46)

When the Son of Man comes in his glory, and all the angels with him, he will sit on his throne in heavenly glory. All the nations will be gathered before him, and he will separate the people one from another as a shepherd separates the sheep from the goats. He will put the sheep on his right and the goats on his left. Then the King will say to those on his right, "Come, you who are blessed by my Father; take your inheritance, the kingdom prepared for you since the creation of the world. For I was hungry and you gave me something to eat, I was thirsty and you gave me something to drink, I was a stranger and you invited me in, I needed clothes and you clothed me, I was sick and you looked after me, I was in prison and you came to visit me." Then the righteous will answer him, "Lord, when did we see you hungry and feed you, or thirsty and give you something to drink? When did we see you a stranger and invite you in, or needing clothes and clothe you? When did we see you sick or in prison and go to visit you?"

The King will reply, "I tell you the truth, whatever you did for one of the least of these brothers of mine, you did for me." Then he will say to those on his left, "Depart from me, you who are cursed, into the eternal fire prepared for the devil and his angels. For I was hungry and you gave me nothing to eat, I was thirsty and you gave me nothing to drink, I was a stranger and you did not invite me in, I needed clothes and you did not clothe me, I was sick and in prison and you did not look after me." They also will answer, "Lord, when did we see you hungry or thirsty or a stranger or needing clothes or sick or in prison, and did not help you?" He will reply, "I tell you the truth, whatever you did not do for one of the least of these, you did not do for me." Then they will go away to eternal punishment, but the righteous to eternal life.

1 Why are the 'sheep' (the righteous) rewarded for their behaviour?
2 How are the 'sheep' rewarded?
3 Why are the 'goats' punished for their behaviour?
4 What is the punishment for the 'goats'?
5 a What do you think this parable is teaching Christians about the way in which they are to behave to please God?
  b How would you expect this belief to influence the way in which Christians live their lives?

Task 3

A cross   A crucifix

1 What is the major difference between a cross and a crucifix?
2 How does the symbol of the crucifix link to the suffering and death of Jesus?
3 How does the symbol of the cross link to the Christian belief in the resurrection of the body and the life everlasting?

Task 4

'You cannot be a Christian without believing in life after death.' Do you agree? Give reasons for your answer, showing that you have thought about more than one point of view.

Topic 1

What is the Bible?

What is...?

The word 'testament' means 'covenant'. A covenant is an agreement. Christians and Jews believe there is a covenant between God and humanity. Moses brought the 'old covenant' (testament). Christians accept that Jesus brought the 'new covenant', (testament).

Activity

Look at page 4. What do Jews and Christians understand by the title 'Messiah'?

The **Bible** is not one book. It is a collection of 66 books, written over many centuries. There are two separate sections to the Bible: the Old Testament and the New Testament.

The Old Testament contains 39 books that are accepted by both Jews and Christians. Christians, alone, accept the 27 books of the New Testament. This is because Jews do not accept Jesus as the Messiah, and the New Testament teaches that Jesus is the Messiah.

The Old Testament

The Old Testament tells of God's agreement with his chosen people, the Jews. These first five books are called the **Pentateuch**, which means the 'first five books'. The first two books are **Genesis**, which begins with an account of Creation, and **Exodus**, which describes how Moses rescued the Hebrews from slavery in Egypt and led them to the Promised Land. The other three books, **Leviticus**, **Numbers** and **Deuteronomy**, contain laws. These five books are called the **Torah** in Judaism.

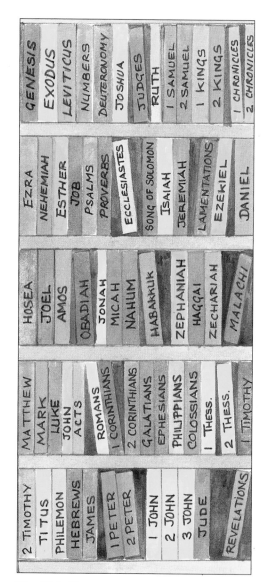

The Bible library

Activity

1 Draw a bookshelf in your book.
2 Copy the books of the Bible on to your bookshelf.

The next twelve books chart the history of the Jews and their relationship with God. They show how, although people turned away from God and broke their promises to him, God never gave up on people, as he still loved them.

The books of the Prophets in the Old Testament explain that God is going to send a special messenger, called the Messiah. One prophet, Micah, says that the Messiah will be born in Bethlehem. Another prophet, Isaiah, says that the Messiah will be a descendant of King David. The Prophets' message was that the Messiah will:

- be born in Bethlehem
- be descended from King David
- be called Emmanuel, which means 'God is with us'
- will heal people
- will tell the poor people about God
- will be especially interested in the poor and the under-privileged
- will act like a servant, even though he was a king
- will care about people, and look after them
- will suffer
- will never do anything wrong.

The other books of the Old Testament are called the **Writings**. These are the books of poetry and wisdom. They include the **Psalms**, and **Proverbs**. The book of Psalms contains prayers and hymns of praise. Christians use psalms from this book as devotional songs in their worship. One of the most popular is Psalm 23, 'The Lord is my shepherd'. The book of Proverbs is a collection of wise sayings.

What is...?

A **prophet** is someone who delivers and explains God's message. A prophet also warns what will happen to those who ignore God's wishes.

Activity

1 List the Old Testament prophecies about the expected Messiah in your book.
2 Tick any prophecies in the list that could refer to Jesus.

What do you think?

What do you think the following proverbs from the Old Testament mean?

'A gossip betrays a confidence' (gives away secrets) (Proverbs 11: 13).

'A gentle answer turns away wrath (anger), but a harsh word stirs up anger' (Proverbs 15: 1).

'Pride goes before destruction (disaster), and a haughty spirit (arrogance) before a fall' (Proverbs 16: 18).

Questions

1 Name the two major divisions of the Bible.
2 What does the word 'testament' mean?
3 Why do you think that Christians have the Jewish scriptures as part of their Bible?
4 a What is a psalm?
  b How are psalms used as part of Christian worship?
5 'Jesus is the Messiah spoken of by the Old Testament prophets.' Do you agree? Give reasons for your answer, showing that you have thought about more than one point of view.

Topic 2
The New Testament

What Is...?

An **evangelist** is someone who spreads the Christian message.

The New Testament tells of the new covenant between God and humanity brought by Jesus. It accepts that Jesus is the Messiah. The themes of the New Testament are the 'Good News' (**Gospel**) of Jesus and his relationship with God and with the people. Christians believe that by following Jesus people can be saved from the punishments they deserve for their sins and be with God forever, after death.

The Gospels

The first four books of the New Testament are the **Gospels** of Matthew, Mark, Luke and John.

These four writers are known as the **evangelists** because they are preaching the message of Jesus.

The 'good news' of the Gospels is that God so loves the world that he has sent his son to lead people back to him. The three gospels of Matthew, Mark and Luke are called the **Synoptic Gospels.** This is because they describe the events of Jesus' life from the same point of view and have a lot in common. John's Gospel explains that the eternal word of God came into the world in human form as Jesus. The message of John is that if people have faith in Jesus as the Son of God then they may achieve eternal life.

A Greek Orthodox priest with the Gospels

The Acts of the Apostles, the Epistles and the Revelations of St John

The **Acts of the Apostles** is an account of how the early church developed. It includes the events of the first Pentecost, when Christians believe the disciples received the gifts of the Holy Spirit, and began to spread the Christian message.

The **Epistles**, or letters, form most of the New Testament. These are the earliest-known Christian writings. The letters are instructions or guidance to the early churches, at places such as Rome and Corinth, to help them to live a Christian life. St Paul wrote most of the letters. In the letters, Paul explains how to behave according to the message of God brought by Jesus.

The Revelations of St John is the last book of the New Testament. The book is believed to be a vision of the end of time, the **Apocalypse**. The revelation is a description of what the writer believed will be the final struggle between good and evil. The writer believes that good will triumph over evil and Christ will return to establish God's kingdom on earth.

 What is ...?

A **martyr** is a person who is put to death for refusing to deny a faith or belief.

A **conversion** takes place when a person changes his or her beliefs or opinions.

 What do you think?

Do you think that there will be a time when the world will end? Discuss your view with other members of the class.

Activity

1. Look back at page 18.
2. Explain the differences and similarities between the Christian understanding of the Apocalypse and the Day of Judgement.

The Apocrypha

Apocrypha means 'hidden things'. The Apocrypha is a collection of fifteen books whose authority is disputed. These books are called the Apocrypha because they are not thought to be equal to the other books of the Bible. The books of the Apocrypha include the Wisdom of Solomon, Ecclesiasticus and Maccabees, and are thought useful as they contain moral and uplifting stories, which can help people to live a good Christian life. Roman Catholics include the Apocrypha with the other books of the Old Testament. Some Bibles include the Apocrypha as a separate section between the Old Testament and the New Testament. Many Protestants do not regard these books as part of the Bible and will not include them anywhere in the Bible.

 **Questions**

1. What does the word 'gospel' mean?
2. Name the four Gospels.
3. Why are the Gospels so important to Christians?
4. Which book in the New Testament describes the history of the early Christian Church?
5. What are the earliest-known Christian writings?
6. How did these early writings come into existence?
7. Do you think a belief in the Apocalypse will influence the way in which Christians live their lives? Give reasons for your answer, showing that you have thought about more than one point of view.

Topic 3

The uses of the Bible

A priest reading the lesson from a lectern during a service

Christians use the Bible in both public and private worship. The reasons why Christians read the Bible include:

- to try to find out more about their faith
- to find ideals for living as God would wish
- to try to hear the voice of God within them as they meditate or pray, as a guide for life.

In church services, there are readings from both the Old and the New Testaments. These readings are called **lessons**, because the Bible passage is teaching people about the Christian faith. The Bible rests on a stand called a **lectern**. During the service, members of the congregation will read the lesson at the lectern.

To make sure that the same readings are not used at every service, and that the readings are suitable for the time of year, many churches use a calendar of readings called a **lectionary**. The lectionary will give a selection of suitable readings from the Old and the New Testament for Sundays, festivals and other special holy days.

What is...?

A **sermon** is a talk or preaching about the Christian way of life. It is given during the service to help the congregation think about what it means to be a Christian.

A minister preaches a sermon from the pulpit

The sermon during a service is usually based on the Bible passage read in the lesson. Its purpose is to help the congregation understand how the passage relates to the Christian faith. The sermon is given from a raised platform called a **pulpit**.

3: The Bible

Activity

Choose a Bible passage you have studied, and write a short sermon to present to the rest of the class to explain the Christian meaning of the passage you have chosen.

In worship, the Bible is used as a source of prayers, such as the Lord's Prayer, and psalms are used as devotional songs to praise God. Many hymns are based on psalms, or Bible passages.

Christians will meet together in small groups for Bible-study classes. The group will read and think about chosen passages from the Bible then discuss the passages to develop their understanding.

The Bible is also used for personal study and meditation. Christians might set aside time each day for prayer and study. They might just open the Bible at random, or work through particular sections using Bible-reading notes. These notes guide them through passages and comment on them. After reading the Bible, Christians will think about what they have read, and perhaps say a prayer. Besides finding out information about their faith, Christians hope to sense the inner guidance of God through reading the words of scripture.

A Bible-study group

What do you think?

'The Bible is outdated. There is no point in studying it.' Do you agree? Give reasons for your answer, showing that you have thought about more than one point of view.

Questions

1 Explain **three** uses of the Bible in a public act of worship.
2 What is a 'lesson'?
3 a What is a lectern?
   b What is the lectern used for in a church?
4 a What is a sermon?
   b How are the sermon and lesson often linked in a service?
5 a What is a lectionary?
   b What is the lectionary used for?
6 Why do Christians study the Bible?
7 'It does not matter if a priest or minister does not study the Bible.' Do you agree? Give reasons for your answer, showing that you have thought about more than one point of view.

Topic 4

The Bible as the Word of God

What is...?

Authority means the person or body having the right to require obedience.

What is...?

Literal means what is said is true. There is no exaggeration, and the meaning is exactly as stated.

Inspired means that something appears to have been influenced by a supernatural source. In the case of the Bible this source is God.

Interpreted means to explain something so that the meaning is made clear.

Christians agree that God inspired the Bible. It is one way by which God has made himself known to the world. Christians agree the Bible is in some way the Word of God, but do not agree that the Bible is the only source of knowledge from God to explain how to live by God's laws.

Protestants accept only the Bible as the **authority** for their Christian belief and practice. Protestants believe that individuals can read and understand the Bible for themselves because the Holy Spirit will guide them to the correct meaning.

Roman Catholics believe that there are other authorities besides the Bible for their Christian belief and practices. They accept that God has also spoken through inspired individuals and the traditions of the Church. Roman Catholics believe that an oral tradition has been passed down from Jesus, through the Apostles, to the Church. This oral tradition is an additional source of authority to the Bible. It provides the leaders with the extra knowledge that needs to be added to the biblical message. The Bible has to be interpreted by the Church leaders for it to be understood correctly. The leaders then explain the message to the members of the Church.

All Christians agree that God has inspired the Bible but Christians do not agree on the interpretation of the message the Bible contains.

Fundamentalist Christians believe that the Bible is the only authority because it is the **direct Word of God**, dictated to the writers as if by a heavenly voice, and therefore everything in the Bible is the literal truth. Since the Bible states that the world was created in six days, Fundamentalists believe in a six-day creation. Fundamentalists argue that if the Bible appears to contradict science, then it is science that is wrong. As the Bible is the Word of God then there are no errors in it since God has guided the writers.

Other Christians believe that the writers of the Bible did not record God's message word for word but brought their personalities and writing styles to each event. These Christians believe that **the Bible is the Word of God interpreted**. For example, they would say that the Bible does not give an exact account of creation, but is a guide to help humans understand God's role in creation. It is a book about faith and knowledge of God; it is not intended to be a scientific textbook. These Christians believe the Bible contains **truths inspired by God**.

A third attitude to the Bible is more **liberal**. These Christians believe that the writers were human beings capable of making mistakes, influenced by ideas around them at the time. They believe that as the writers of the Bible were concerned with the people and events of their time, modern readers

need to reinterpret the Bible's ideas in the light of modern understanding of the world in order to reveal aspects of God. For example, these Christians regard the story of Adam and Eve as no more than symbolic poetry to help people understand God's part in creation.

Many Christians may combine some conservative views of the Bible with liberal ones. For example, they may reject the six-day account of creation but not the physical resurrection of Jesus.

 ## What do you think?

Did God create Adam and Eve?

Activity

Explain the different understandings of the Bible as the Word of God in your book.

 ## Questions

1 What do Christians understand by the description of the Bible as 'the Word of God'?

2 How do Protestants believe that they are guided to the correct understanding of the biblical message?

3 What extra source of authority besides the Bible is found in the Roman Catholic Church?

4 a How do Fundamentalists understand the term 'the Word of God'?

   b How do Fundamentalists understand the Creation account in Genesis?

5 a How would other Christians understand the Bible as the interpreted Word of God?

   b How would these Christians understand the Creation account in Genesis?

6 a What is a liberal view of the Bible as the Word of God?

   b How would liberal Christians understand the Creation account in Genesis?

7 'It does not matter if you do not accept the biblical account of creation.' Do you agree? Give reasons for your answer, showing that you have thought about more than one point of view.

Do you understand...

the Christian attitude to the Bible?

Task 1

'The Old Testament has no relevance for a Christian.' Do you agree? Give reasons for your answer, showing that you have thought about more than one point of view.

Task 2

The Feeding of the Five Thousand is a description in the Gospels of one of the miracles of Jesus. A **miracle** is an event that does not conform to the known scientific laws. It appears to be a supernatural event.

The feeding of the five thousand (Mark 6:30–44)

The apostles gathered around Jesus and reported to him all they had done and taught. Then, because so many people were coming and going that they did not even have a chance to eat, he said to them, "Come with me by yourselves to a quiet place and get some rest." So they went away by themselves in a boat to a solitary place. But many who saw them leaving recognized them and ran on foot from all the towns and got there ahead of them. When Jesus landed and saw a large crowd, he had compassion on them, because they were like sheep without a shepherd. So he began teaching them many things. By this time it was late in the day, so his disciples came to him. "This is a remote place," they said, "and it's already very late. Send the people away so they can go to the surrounding countryside and villages and buy themselves something to eat." But he answered, "You give them something to eat." They said to him, "That would take eight months of a man's wages! Are we to go and spend that much on bread and give it to them to eat?" "How many loaves do you have?" he asked. "Go and see." When they found out, they said, "Five – and two fish." Then Jesus directed them to have all the people sit down in groups on the green grass. So they sat down in groups of hundreds and fifties. Taking the five loaves and the two fish and looking up to heaven, he gave thanks and broke the loaves. Then he gave them to his disciples to set before the people. He also divided the two fish among them all. They all ate and were satisfied, and the disciples picked up twelve basketfuls of broken pieces of bread and fish. The number of the men who had eaten was five thousand.

1   This passage is taken from the Gospel of St Mark. What good news do you think a Christian would believe that this passage brings?
2   Suggest **two** different ways in which Christians may understand Mark's Gospel as 'The Word of God'.
3   Not all Christians accept the Feeding of the Five Thousand as a miracle. What other explanation could be given to account for everyone who was present having enough food to eat?
4   Why do you think that many churches hold regular Bible-study classes?

Task 3

Christians often take their own copies of the Bible to church services and follow the Bible readings in the service.

1   Why do you think that Christians will want to take their Bible to church with them?
2   Why do the four Gospels have special authority for Christians?
3   Why do Christians read the New Testament regularly?
4   Why do you think many churches hold regular Bible-study classes?
5   How might the Bible help a Christian to worship in private?
6   'It does not matter how the Bible is interpreted so long as it is read.' Do you agree? Give reasons for your answer, showing that you have thought about more than one point of view.

Task 4

Each of the four Gospels of Matthew, Mark, Luke and John has an account of the Resurrection of Jesus. There are variations between the four versions. How do you think a Fundamentalist Christian and a Liberal Christian would explain the differences between the four Gospel accounts? (Read the four different versions to help you to answer this question.)

Topic 1

The Christian year

Activity

Copy the outline of the Christian Church year into your book and colour in the sections.

The major festivals in the Church year remember important events in the life of Jesus. These events have shaped the Christian calendar.

What do you think?

Which events in the life of Jesus do you think are going to be the most important ones for Christians?

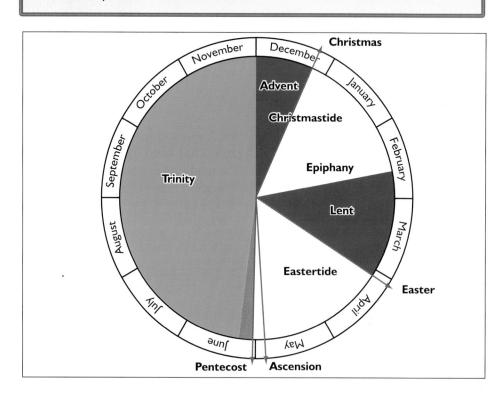

The Christian Church year

Advent

The Christian Church year **begins** with Advent. Advent starts on the fourth Sunday before Christmas Day and ends at midnight on Christmas Eve. The colour of Advent is **purple** because purple is a colour used to express sorrow, and Advent was the time when Christians used **to show God that they were sorry for their sins**. There was no music in church at this time and weddings were not allowed. People fasted.

Advent is a season rather than a festival. It is a time of **waiting and preparing** for the **birth of Christ** (the Messiah) at Christmas and **his return at the end of time**. The word 'advent' means 'coming'. Christians remember during Advent that God sent Jesus to save the world from sin.

Christians believe that when Adam and Eve disobeyed God in the Garden of Eden, sin came into the world. People became separated from God. God still loved people although they had disobeyed him. He sent Jesus to open the way back to God and to show people how to be obedient to God so that sin and death could be conquered. Jesus is seen as the **Light of the World** bringing people out of the darkness of sin.

The **Bible-readings** in church services will be suitable for the season and include readings from the Old Testament which look forward to (prophesy) the coming of the Messiah (Christ). The prophet Isaiah said that the Messiah would be a descendant of King David. Isaiah said the Messiah would be wise, defend the humble and weak and bring justice into the world. The Messiah would be a servant of humanity, not a warrior. Other passages are read which describe the birth and work of John the Baptist as he prepared for the coming of the Messiah. Christians also remember the **Annunciation**, which is celebrated in March. The Annunciation is when the Angel Gabriel came to tell Mary that she was to be the mother of God's son.

An Advent crown

Christians **count down** to Christmas during Advent. This has led to several customs to help the count-down to Christmas, such as the Advent crown.

The Advent crown has four purple or red candles. One is lit on the fourth Sunday before Christmas Day; two are lit on the third Sunday, three on the second Sunday and all four on the last Sunday before Christmas Day. The crown is made of holly. Christians believe the holly represents the crown of thorns that was placed on Jesus' head at his crucifixion, and the red berries symbolise his blood shed for their sins.

Activity

The most famous way to count down to Christmas is to use an Advent calendar. Behind each of the 24 doors of the calendar there is a symbol linked to the birth of Jesus. Behind the 24th door is a picture of Mary, Joseph and the baby Jesus. Design an Advent calendar that would be suitable for a Christian to use.

Questions

1 a Which season begins the Church year?
  b How long does this season last?
2 Why is purple the colour associated with Advent?
3 What **two** events associated with Jesus are Christians preparing for at this time?
4 Why is this season important to Christians?
5 'Advent is no longer a time of preparation for Jesus' birth.' Do you agree? Give reasons for your answer, showing that you have thought about more than one point of view.

What is...?

The Nativity is the name given to the birth of Jesus.

The Magi is another name used to describe the wise men who followed the star to visit Jesus.

The first Christmas

Christmas celebrates the birth of Jesus. **Nativity plays** teach Christians the story of Jesus' birth found in the Gospel accounts. They originated at a time when most people could not read the Christmas story for themselves. Nativity plays are still performed in schools and churches to continue the tradition of teaching the story. The events of the first Christmas are acted out to help children learn the story and to remind adults of what happened. The Gospels of Matthew and Luke have accounts of the birth of Jesus.

Nativity plays are still performed

Matthew's version of the Nativity (Matthew 1:18–2:15)

This is how the birth of Jesus Christ came about: His mother Mary was pledged to be married to Joseph, but before they came together, she was found to be with child through the Holy Spirit.

Because Joseph her husband was a righteous man and did not want to expose her to public disgrace, he had in mind to divorce her quietly. But after he had considered this, an angel of the Lord appeared to him in a dream and said, "Joseph son of David, do not be afraid to take Mary home as your wife, because what is conceived in her is from the Holy Spirit. She will give birth to a son, and you are to give him the name Jesus, because he will save his people from their sins."

All this took place to fulfil what the Lord had said through the prophet: "The virgin will be with child and will give birth to a son, and they will call him Immanuel" – which means, "God with us."

When Joseph woke up, he did what the angel of the Lord had commanded him and took Mary home as his wife. But he had no union with her until she gave birth to a son. And he gave him the name Jesus.

After Jesus was born in Bethlehem in Judea, during the time of King Herod, Magi from the east came to Jerusalem and asked, "Where is the one who has been born king of the Jews? We saw his star in the east and have come to worship him." When King Herod heard this he was disturbed, and all Jerusalem with him. When he had called together all the people's chief priests and teachers of the law, he asked them where the Christ was to be born. "In Bethlehem in Judea," they replied, "for this is what the prophet has written: 'But you, Bethlehem, in the land of Judah, are by no means least among the rulers of Judah; for out of you will come a ruler who will be the shepherd of my people Israel.'" Then Herod called the Magi secretly and found out from them the exact time the star had appeared. He sent them to Bethlehem and said, "Go and make a careful search for the child. As soon as you find him, report to me, so that I too may go and worship him." After they had heard the king, they went on their way, and the star they had seen in the east went ahead of them until it stopped over the place where the child was. When they saw the star, they were overjoyed. On coming to the house, they saw the child with his mother Mary, and they bowed down and worshipped him. Then they opened their treasures and presented him with gifts of gold and of incense and of myrrh. And having been warned in a dream not to go back to Herod, they returned to their country by another route.

When they had gone, an angel of the Lord appeared to Joseph in a dream. "Get up," he said, "take the child and his mother and escape to Egypt. Stay there until I tell you, for Herod is going to search for the child to kill him." So he got up, took the child and his mother during the night and left for Egypt, where he stayed until the death of Herod. And so was fulfilled what the Lord had said through the prophet: "Out of Egypt I called my son."

What is...?

A **census** is an official count of a population.

The **crib** is another way in which Christians are reminded of the events of the first Christmas. The crib refers to the stable where Jesus was born. It includes figures representing Mary, Joseph, the shepherds, the wise men and the angels. The baby Jesus is often not placed in the manger until midnight on Christmas Eve.

The crib scene is a reminder of the Christmas story

Luke's version of the Nativity (Luke 2:1–20)

In those days Caesar Augustus issued a decree that a census should be taken of the entire Roman world. (This was the first census that took place while Quirinius was governor of Syria.) And everyone went to his own town to register. So Joseph also went up from the town of Nazareth in Galilee to Judea, to Bethlehem the town of David, because he belonged to the house and line of David. He went there to register with Mary, who was pledged to be married to him and was expecting a child. While they were there, the time came for the baby to be born, and she gave birth to her firstborn, a son. She wrapped him in cloths and placed him in a manger, because there was no room for them in the inn. And there were shepherds living out in the fields nearby, keeping watch over their flocks at night. An angel of the Lord appeared to them, and the glory of the Lord shone around them, and they were terrified. But the angel said to them, "Do not be afraid. I bring you good news of great joy that will be for all the people. Today in the town of David a Saviour has been born to you; he is Christ the Lord. This will be a sign to you: You will find a baby wrapped in cloths and lying in a manger." Suddenly a great company of the heavenly host appeared with the angel, praising God and saying, "Glory to God in the highest, and on earth peace to men on whom his favour rests."

Activity

Using the accounts of Jesus' birth in Matthew and Luke, imagine that you are a newspaper reporter covering the story of the birth of Jesus for *The Bethlehem Times*. Write a newspaper account of the events surrounding Jesus' birth. Try to include some of your thoughts, feelings and reactions to what you have seen and heard.

Carol-singing is a method that Christians use to teach the Christmas message and remember the events of the first Christmas. Carol-singing in churches and in streets is a popular custom at Christmas. Carols are songs which either tell the story of Jesus' birth, such as 'Once in Royal David's City', or the meaning of his birth, such as 'Love came down at Christmas'. Salvation Army bands often play carols in shopping centres to raise money for the less fortunate and to remind people of the true meaning of Christmas. Carol-singing links back to the angels coming to tell the shepherds of the birth of Jesus and singing praises to God.

Activity

Draw a Christmas tree, decorated with a star, angel, candles, and presents. Look back at the Christmas story and say what you think each of the decorations represents.

What do you think?

Christmas trees are evergreens. The fact that it is a tree and evergreen has a meaning linked to the Christmas message for Christians. What do you think the tree represents for Christians?

Questions

1 a What do Christians celebrate on Christmas Day?
   b Explain why Christmas Day is an important festival for Christians.
2 What does the Apostles' Creed teach about the birth of Jesus?
3 How do Nativity plays, cribs and carol-singing help Christians remember the events of the first Christmas?
4 Why do you think many Christians use carol-singing to raise money for charity?

Activity

Find out as much as you can about the Orthodox celebration of Christmas. Write a detailed description of the Orthodox celebration of Christmas.

Christmas means **Christ's Mass**. The name 'Christmas' reminds Christians of the special Holy Communion service to remember God coming to earth in human form as Jesus. When Christians receive the bread and wine, they are reminded that Jesus was born to die to save the world from the punishment for sin. **Midnight Mass** is the most important Christmas celebration for many Christians. The Mass starts at 11.30 pm on Christmas Eve. The carols during the service will express the Christian joy at Jesus' birth. The Bible-readings will remind the congregation of the events of the first Christmas and the meaning of these events for Christians. At midnight, the figure of the baby Jesus will be placed in the manger in the crib scene to show that Jesus has arrived. If the church has bells then they will be rung to celebrate Jesus' birth.

What is ...?

Commercialisation means to exploit or spoil something for the purpose of making a profit.

What do you think?

Many Christians believe that most people have forgotten the true message of Christmas. They believe that manufacturers and shops have commercialised Christmas. People are only interested in enjoying themselves by eating, drinking and exchanging presents rather than thinking of others as Jesus intended. Do you agree with this Christian view? Give reasons for your answer, showing that you have thought about more than one point of view.

 Activity

Look at page 37. What happened when the wise men (Magi) visited Jesus?

The Magi brought three gifts to Jesus

Epiphany

Epiphany means 'manifestation' or to 'show forth'. The feast of Epiphany is celebrated on **6 January,** as this is when the wise men were thought to have visited Jesus. Christians believe that this is one of the ways God showed the world that Jesus was his son.

There is no mention in Matthew's Gospel of how many wise men there were. The Orthodox Church sets the number at twelve, but the Western churches accept three. This is because Matthew refers to three gifts. Gradually Western tradition has turned the wise men into kings, with the names Caspar, a young European; Melchior, a middle-aged Asian; and Balthasar, an elderly African. In this way, Christians are demonstrating that Jesus came to save all ages and nations of the world. The three gifts brought by the Magi were gold, frankincense and myrrh. Each gift brought by the Magi has a symbolic message linked to the belief that Jesus is the Son of God and Saviour of the world:

- gold is the sign of Kingship, and Christians accept Jesus as their Lord;
- frankincense is used in worship and Christians worship Jesus;
- myrrh was a spice used to anoint leaders and to prepare dead bodies for burial. Christians call Jesus, 'Christ', meaning the anointed one of God chosen to die for the sins of the world.

The celebration of Epiphany

Nonconformist churches tend to ignore the festival except during the ordinary Sunday services close to Epiphany. The hymns, sermon and Bible-readings will remember the event.

Orthodox, Roman Catholic and **Anglican** churches hold a special Eucharist (service of Holy Communion) on 6 January. The Bible-readings will be incidents which show that Jesus is God in human form (**incarnation**), and God's son. The Bible-readings include:

- the visit of the wise men (page 37)
- Jesus lost in the temple when he was 12 years old (page 54)
- the baptism of Jesus (page 42)
- the first miracle of Jesus at the marriage in Cana (page 91).

Activity

1 Study the biblical accounts of events in the life of Jesus read in church during Epiphany.

2 For each event, explain why Christians believe that it shows Jesus to be the Son of God.

Questions

1 Which festival does Epiphany follow?
2 What does the word 'Epiphany' mean?
3 **a** Outline the events which took place when the Magi visited Jesus.
  b What is the importance of Epiphany for Christians?
4 State and explain the meaning for Christians of each of the three gifts brought by the wise men.
5 Why do you think that Christianity had developed the tradition that the three wise men represent the three ages and races of humankind?

Topic 3 — Lent

In Britain, the day **before** the beginning of Lent is called **Shrove Tuesday**. The word 'shrove' comes from 'shrive', meaning to be free from sin after confession. It used to be the day on which Christians confessed their sins to God and prepared for Lent. During Lent, Christians remember the 40 days Jesus spent in the wilderness fasting after his baptism. At the end of the 40 days he was tempted by Satan to use his powers from God for himself. Jesus refused to give into temptation and Christians believe that they must try to do the same.

The baptism and temptation of Jesus (Mark 1:1–13)

At that time Jesus came from Nazareth in Galilee and was baptized by John in the Jordan. As Jesus was coming up out of the water, he saw heaven being torn open and the Spirit descending on him like a dove. And a voice came from heaven: "You are my Son, whom I love; with you I am well pleased." At once the Spirit sent him out into the desert, and he was in the desert forty days, being tempted by Satan. He was with the wild animals, and angels attended him.

The colour of Lent is purple because Lent is a time when people show God that they are sorry for their sins. Lent is a season of soul-searching and repentance for Christians as they prepare for Easter. The preparation during Lent has three aspects: fasting, prayer and good works.

Fasting – During Lent, Christians try to follow Jesus' example of not giving into temptation by giving up something they enjoy, such as chocolate. By giving up something Christians are showing thanks to God for his many gifts. It is a way of getting closer to God and sharing a little of Jesus' suffering on Good Friday. Christians believe fasting helps to strengthen an individual's ability to overcome temptations.

What do you think?

'I've given up chocolate for Lent but one small bar won't hurt me.' Do you think a Christian would agree with this attitude? Give reasons for your opinion, showing that you have thought about more than one point of view.

Prayer – There will be extra acts of worship during Lent, both public and private. Christians give extra time to reading the Bible or attending special prayer services on weekdays. There will be many ecumenical services. An ecumenical service is when different denominations worship together. These services act as a reminder that Christians are part of the same faith and one family in God. Many churches hold Lenten courses, which are a series of weekly meetings throughout Lent to give people the opportunity to learn more about the Christian faith.

Good works – Jesus was hungry after he had fasted for 40 days. Satan tempted him to turn the stones into bread. Jesus refused to do this as he was to use his powers to help people in need not himself. Christians try to do the same during Lent. Many churches hold fundraising events or hold hunger lunches. At a hunger lunch, Christians meet in fellowship at lunchtime and fast. The money saved from not eating a lunch is donated to charities that provide food for the hungry people of the world.

Ash Wednesday – this is the first day of Lent. The name Ash Wednesday comes from a service in the Roman Catholic Church, and some Anglican churches at which ash is used made from the burnt palm crosses from the previous year. At the end of the service, the sign of the Cross is made on people's foreheads with the ash, as a sign that people are sorry for their sins and want to be forgiven by God. The ashes give the idea of a new beginning after the old ways have been destroyed. During the service, the words used in a funeral are spoken: '**earth to earth, ashes to ashes, dust to dust**'. Christians are reminded of the belief that Jesus, by his death on the cross on Good Friday, gave people the chance of a new start by following his example. Jesus had opened the way back to God.

? Questions

1 a What is the day before the beginning of Lent called in Britain?
  b How did this day get its name?
2 a What name is given to the first day of Lent?
  b How did this day get its name?
  c What is the importance of this day for many Christians?
3 a What event in the life of Jesus is remembered during Lent?
  b Why is this event important to Christians?
4 a What are the **three** aspects of preparation for Easter during Lent?
  b Explain what each of these three aspects involves. Support your answer with examples.

Topic 4 — Holy Week

Holy Week is the last week of Lent. During this week Christians remember the events of the last week of the earthly life of Jesus, as he prepared for his death on the cross on **Good Friday**. Holy Week begins on **Palm Sunday** and ends at midnight on **Holy Saturday** (the day before Easter). There are special acts of worship during the week linked to the events that took place in Jesus' life during that week.

Activity

Draw a timeline of the major events in the life of Jesus that took place during Holy Week, based on the information on pages 44 to 49.

Palm Sunday is the first day of Holy Week. Christians remember that it was on this day that Jesus rode in triumph into Jerusalem on a donkey.

Jesus rode into Jerusalem (Mark 11:1–10)

As they approached Jerusalem and came to Bethphage and Bethany at the Mount of Olives, Jesus sent two of his disciples, saying to them, "Go to the village ahead of you, and just as you enter it, you will find a colt tied there, which no one has ever ridden. Untie it and bring it here. If anyone asks you, 'Why are you doing this?' tell him, 'The Lord needs it and will send it back here shortly.'"

They went and found a colt outside in the street, tied at a doorway. As they untied it, some people standing there asked, "What are you doing, untying that colt?" They answered as Jesus had told them to, and the people let them go. When they brought the colt to Jesus and threw their cloaks over it, he sat on it. Many people spread their cloaks on the road, while others spread branches they had cut in the fields. Those who went ahead and those who followed shouted, "Hosanna!" "Blessed is he who comes in the name of the Lord!" "Blessed is the coming kingdom of our father David!" "Hosanna in the highest!"

In many Western churches the congregation are given palm crosses. The palm crosses are a reminder that people greeted Jesus as the Messiah by placing palm branches on the ground in front of him. The shape of a cross reminds Christians that Jesus was riding to his death at the end of the week. In some churches people act out the events of Palm Sunday and sing hymns, such as 'Ride on, Ride on in Majesty'.

What do you think?

'It helps people to celebrate a Christian festival more easily if they have a special symbol for that day, such as palm crosses.' Do you agree? Give reasons for your answer, showing that you have thought about more than one point of view.

On the **Monday** of Holy Week, Jesus returned to Jerusalem. When he entered the temple, he saw traders selling goods and exchanging money. He was angry and threw them out. He said, 'My house shall be called a house of prayer but you have made it a den of thieves'. He meant that the traders did not have the right attitude to the place of worship.

On **Tuesday**, Jesus was questioned many times by the leaders as they tried to trick him into saying something for which they could arrest him. It was on this day that Jesus gave what Christians consider to be the greatest commandment, '**To love God with all your heart, mind, soul and strength and to love your neighbour as yourself**'.

Christians receive palm crosses on Palm Sunday

What do you think?

What do you think Jesus was teaching people about the way they should live their lives when he gave his followers the 'greatest' commandment?

Questions

1　a　What is the last week of Lent called?
　　b　Why do you think that it is given this name?
2　a　What event in the life of Jesus is remembered on Palm Sunday?
　　b　Why is this event important to Christians?
3　a　What is the greatest commandment?
　　b　Do you think that Christians would think it important to follow this commandment? Give reasons for your answer, showing that you have thought about more than one point of view.

4: Christian festivals

What is...?

Chrism is an oil used for anointing in the Roman Catholic and Orthodox churches.

On **Wednesday** of Holy Week, Jesus stayed at the home of Simon the Leper in Bethany. A woman entered and poured valuable perfumed oil over the feet of Jesus. She wiped it away with her hair. Judas Iscariot was angry. He said that the oil could have been sold and the money given to the poor. Jesus said that she had done a beautiful thing as she had prepared him for his burial. The poor would always be with them but he would soon be leaving them. Judas did not understand and went to the authorities to betray Jesus. He was paid 30 pieces of silver. In the **Roman Catholic Church** the oils of chrism left over from the previous year are burnt. On Maundy Thursday the new oils for the coming year are consecrated.

Maundy Thursday is the day on which Jesus gave his followers a new commandment, 'to love one another'. 'Maundy' means commandment. Jesus showed that everyone was equal and to show this he washed the feet of his disciples. **The Last Supper** followed the washing of the feet. During the meal, Jesus blessed the bread and wine. He gave it to his followers and said that they were to represent his body and blood given for the forgiveness of sins. He told his followers to repeat the ceremony. They were to eat the bread and drink the wine 'in memory of me'.

The Last Supper (Mark 14:18–26)

When evening came, Jesus arrived with the Twelve. While they were reclining at the table eating, he said, "I tell you the truth, one of you will betray me – one who is eating with me."

They were saddened, and one by one they said to him, "Surely not I?" "It is one of the Twelve," he replied, "one who dips bread into the bowl with me. The Son of Man will go just as it is written about him. But woe to that man who betrays the Son of Man! It would be better for him if he had not been born." While they were eating, Jesus took bread, gave thanks and broke it, and gave it to his disciples, saying, "Take it; this is my body." Then he took the cup, gave thanks and offered it to them, and they all drank from it. "This is my blood of the covenant, which is poured out for many," he said to them. "I tell you the truth, I will not drink again of the fruit of the vine until that day when I drink it anew in the kingdom of God." When they had sung a hymn, they went out to the Mount of Olives.

After the meal, Jesus went with his followers to the Garden of Gethsemane. He spent time in prayer while his followers slept. It was here that Judas led the soldiers to Jesus. Jesus was arrested and put on trial.

The Last Supper, as painted by Leonardo da Vinci

Worship on Maundy Thursday

In many Anglican and Roman Catholic churches, the service of foot-washing (**Pedilavium**) is held to remember Jesus' command '**to love one another**'.

Many churches have a special celebration of Holy Communion to remember the Last Supper. This service often includes acting out the events of the night. Many churches remain open after the service is over. Many people hold a vigil to remember that Jesus asked his followers to stay awake with him. The churches are stripped of all decorations in preparation for Good Friday. This day is known as Great Thursday in the Orthodox Church.

What Is ...?

A **vigil** is to stay awake to watch for something.

Questions

1 a What commandment did Jesus give his followers on Maundy Thursday?
  b How did Jesus put this commandment into practice before the Last Supper?
2 Describe the major event of the Last Supper.
3 'Judas deserves to be one of the most hated people in history.' Do you agree? Give reasons for your opinion, showing that you have thought about more than one point of view.

Good Friday

Good Friday is the day on which Jesus 'suffered under Pontius Pilate, was crucified dead and buried'. Pontius Pilate signed Jesus' death warrant and Jesus was nailed to a cross and left hanging there until he died.

Good, or God's, Friday is a sad, solemn day for Christians as it is the day on which they believe Jesus suffered on the cross to gain God's forgiveness for sin. They believe Jesus showed what true obedience to God meant, and made up for Adam and Eve's disobedience (original sin). Christians remember the events of the day and Jesus' words from the cross during special Good Friday services. There will be suitable hymns and Bible-readings. Some choirs perform special music, such as Stainer's 'Crucifixion'. The churches are dark and solemn to show that this is a solemn day in the Church year. There will be times of silence so that Christians can concentrate on Jesus suffering for their sins, especially between noon and 3 pm. Jesus was dying on the cross during this time.

The Fourteen Stations of the Cross

1. PILATE CONDEMNS JESUS TO DEATH.

2. JESUS IS GIVEN THE CROSS.

3. JESUS FALLS UNDER ITS WEIGHT.

4. JESUS MEETS HIS MOTHER, MARY.

5. SIMON OF CYRENE HELPS JESUS CARRY THE CROSS.

6. VERONICA WIPES JESUS' FACE.

7. JESUS FALLS AGAIN.

8. JESUS SPEAKS TO THE WEEPING WOMEN.

9. JESUS FALLS A THIRD TIME.

10. JESUS IS STRIPPED OF HIS GARMENTS.

11. JESUS IS NAILED TO THE CROSS.

12. JESUS DIES ON THE CROSS.

13. JESUS IS TAKEN DOWN FROM THE CROSS.

14. JESUS IS BURIED.

The **Stations of the Cross** are fourteen pictures or statues around the church. Each picture shows an event from Good Friday. Christians move from picture to picture following Jesus' suffering on Good Friday. They will stop at each picture and there will be a reminder of the event shown. There may be a Bible-reading, a prayer or hymn. In Jerusalem, people follow the route Jesus took along the Via Dolerosa (Street of Tears). Many will walk along the route carrying a cross.

After his death, Jesus was placed in the empty tomb of Joseph of Arimathea. The women could not finish the burial rites because the Sabbath was about to begin and no work was allowed. A stone was rolled in front of the tomb. Roman soldiers were put on guard and the followers of Jesus went home.

The burial of Jesus (Mark 15:42–47)

So as evening approached, Joseph of Arimathea, a prominent member of the Council, who was himself waiting for the kingdom of God, went boldly to Pilate and asked for Jesus' body. Pilate was surprised to hear that he was already dead. Summoning the centurion, he asked him if Jesus had already died. When he learned from the centurion that it was so, he gave the body to Joseph. So Joseph bought some linen cloth, took down the body, wrapped it in the linen, and placed it in a tomb cut out of rock. Then he rolled a stone against the entrance of the tomb. Mary Magdalene and Mary the mother of Jesus saw where he was laid.

In the **Orthodox Church,** the day is known as Great Friday. A 'tomb' is made in the middle of the church and surrounded with flowers. A service is held in the early afternoon, when a cloth bearing a life-size image of the dead Christ is carried from the sanctuary round the church and placed on the tomb. The congregation come forward to kiss the painted cloth. Later another service is held and the cloth is carried in procession around the outside of the church. The congregation follow holding candles. It is like a real funeral procession with the people dressed in black as they mourn the death of Jesus.

 Activity

Choose a Christian denomination and find out how the events of Good Friday are remembered. Write a description of this church's Good Friday worship in your book.

 **Questions**

1 a What events in the life of Jesus are remembered on Good Friday?
  b Why are these events important to Christians?
2 The word 'station' means a stopping-place. Why do you think that the fourteen pictures used as part of the Good Friday worship are called the Stations of the Cross?
3 'It does not matter that the shops are open on Good Friday.' Do you agree? Give reasons for your answer, showing that you have thought about more than one point of view.

Topic 5

Easter

Activity

Look at page 16. Why was it necessary for Jesus to 'descend into hell'?

Holy Saturday

Holy Saturday is the day on which Christians believe Jesus 'descended into hell'. People had become separated from God. Jesus had died to open the way back to God.

What do you think?

Do you think that hell exists? Discuss your thoughts about hell with the teacher and the rest of the class.

Easter Sunday

Easter Sunday is the most important day in the Church year. It is the 'third day' after Jesus died. Jesus rose from the dead and was seen by his followers on that day. The women went to the tomb to finish the burial rites. The stone was rolled back and the tomb was empty.

The resurrection of Jesus (Mark 16:1–12)

When the Sabbath was over, Mary Magdalene, Mary the mother of James, and Salome bought spices so that they might go to anoint Jesus' body. Very early on the first day of the week, just after sunrise, they were on their way to the tomb and they asked each other, "Who will roll the stone away from the entrance of the tomb?" But when they looked up, they saw that the stone, which was very large, had been rolled away. As they entered the tomb, they saw a young man dressed in a white robe sitting on the right side, and they were alarmed. "Don't be alarmed," he said. "You are looking for Jesus the Nazarene, who was crucified. He has risen! He is not here. See the place where they laid him. But go, tell his disciples and Peter, 'He is going ahead of you into Galilee. There you will see him, just as he told you.'" Trembling and bewildered, the women went out and fled from the tomb. They said nothing to anyone, because they were afraid. When Jesus rose early on the first day of the week, he appeared first to Mary Magdalene, out of whom he had driven seven demons. She went and told those who had been with him and who were mourning and weeping. When they heard that Jesus was alive and that she had seen him, they did not believe it. Afterward Jesus appeared in a different form to two of them while they were walking in the country.

Activity

In groups try to work out what could have happened to the body of Jesus if he had not risen from the dead. Share your ideas with the rest of the class. Try to think of evidence that will disprove ideas put forward by other groups to explain the empty tomb.

Easter eggs

Easter eggs are used as a Christian symbol to represent the empty tomb. The outside of the egg looks dead but inside there is new life, which is going to break out. The Easter egg is a reminder that Jesus will rise from his tomb and bring new life. Orthodox Christians dye boiled eggs red to represent the blood of Christ shed for the sins of the world. Chocolate Easter eggs became popular because Easter is the end of the Lenten fast.

Easter gardens

Easter gardens are another teaching method used by Christians to explain the events of Easter. They are made out of moss, twigs and stones and remind Christians of the empty tomb on Easter morning.

An Easter garden

Questions

1 a What event in the life of Jesus is remembered at Easter?
  b Why is this event important to Christians?
2 Explain how each of the following symbols helps Christians to remember the meaning of Easter:
  a Easter eggs
  b Easter gardens.
3 Why do you think that Christians regard Easter as the major Christian festival?
4 'Children are given chocolate Easter eggs but not the Christian message.' Do you agree? Give reasons for your answer, showing that you have thought about more than one point of view.

Topic 6 Easter to Pentecost

Activity

1 Find out how Easter is celebrated in the Orthodox Church.
2 Write a description of the Orthodox celebration of Easter in your book.

Christian worship at Easter is a joyful and happy occasion. The churches are decorated with flowers, and the bells ring. Most Christians will try to attend church on this day.

In some Christian churches, Easter worship will begin on **Holy Saturday**. The service will begin at about 11:30 pm. Christians are keeping watch for the Resurrection of Jesus. The first part of the service will be readings from the Gospel of the events of the first Easter.

The Roman Catholic Church and **some Church of England** churches will hold a vigil. The people gather outside around a bonfire. The priest will bless the fire. He will turn to one of the servers who will carry the **Paschal candle**. The Paschal candle is a large candle which is marked with a cross and the first and last letters of the Greek alphabet, alpha and omega. The priest inscribes the current year on to the candle and then inserts five grains of incense into the candle to represent the five wounds Christ received at the crucifixion. The priest will carry the lighted Paschal candle back into the church. He will raise the candle several times as he chants 'Christ our Light'. The people will light smaller candles from the large Paschal candle. A service to celebrate Christ's resurrection follows.

Dawn services

Many Protestants meet together on a hillside at dawn on Easter morning. As the sun rises they remember the women's visit to the tomb. They will sing hymns to show that they are happy that the tomb was empty. A normal Sunday service will follow but the hymns, Bible-readings and sermon will remember the events of the first Easter and its importance for Christians.

Questions

1 a What is a vigil?
  b Why do you think that many Christians want to hold a vigil at Easter?
2 Write a description of an Easter vigil.
3 a Describe a dawn service.
  b Why do you think that many Christians hold a dawn service?
4 What are the common features of Christian worship on Easter Sunday?
5 Why do you think that many Christians attend a service of Holy Communion on Easter Sunday?

Pentecost

Pentecost is celebrated 50 days after Easter and 11 days after Christians believe Jesus returned to heaven on Ascension Day. Pentecost is the day on which the disciples of Jesus received the gifts of the Holy Spirit.

The first Pentecost (Acts 2:1–15)

When the day of Pentecost came, they were all together in one place. Suddenly a sound like the blowing of a violent wind came from heaven and filled all the house where they were sitting. They saw what seemed like tongues of fire that separated and came to rest on each of them. And they were all filled with the Holy Spirit, and began to talk in other tongues, as the Spirit enabled them. Now there were staying in Jerusalem God-fearing Jews from every nation under heaven. When they heard this sound, a crowd came together in bewilderment, because, each one of them heard them speaking in his own language. Utterly amazed, they asked: "Are not all these men who are speaking Galileans? Then how is it that each of us hears them in his own native language?"

The disciples had gathered on the day of Pentecost and a great wind came upon them, filling them with the Holy Spirit. They spoke in many different languages by the power of the Holy Spirit so that all would hear and understand the Gospel that they were proclaiming. Peter taught people the Christian message. They are to **"repent and be baptised everyone of you in the name of Jesus Christ for the remission of sins, and you shall receive the gift of the Holy Spirit"**. Three thousand people were baptised on that day.

The celebration of Pentecost

Pentecost is known as the **birthday of the church.** This is because on this day the disciples began to spread the Christian message. In Britain, this festival is often called Whit Sunday because it was a popular day for baptism at which people wore white clothes.

The festival celebrates the belief that the Holy Spirit brings new life to the believer and changes life for the better. There are special services in churches. The day may include a Whit walk, when the congregation walks around the town or village, stopping at various places to sing a hymn, pray or preach the Christian message. In this way, they are re-enacting the events of the first Pentecost, when the disciples went out to preach Christ's message to the people of Jerusalem. The aim is to bring others to the faith.

? Questions

1 What event is remembered at Pentecost?
2 Why is this event important to Christians?
3 How is the festival of Pentecost celebrated?
4 'I believe in the Holy Spirit.' Explain what Christians believe about the Holy Spirit. (Look at page 19 to help you with your answer.)

Do you understand...
Christian festivals?

Task 1

> Once in Royal David's City
> Stood a lonely cattle shed
> where a mother laid her baby
> in a manger for his bed.
> Mary was that mother mild.
> Jesus Christ her little child.

1 **a** During which season do Christians prepare for Christmas?
  b How might Christians prepare for Christmas?
2 How does the above verse link to the Christmas message?
3 Why might groups of Christians go carol-singing?
4 Choose another way in which Christians celebrate Christmas. Explain what happens and how the celebration links to the Christmas story.
5 'It does not matter if you go carol-singing and keep the money for yourself.' Do you agree? Give reasons for your answer, showing that you have thought about more than one point of view.

Task 2

Jesus lost in the temple
(Luke 2:42–52)

When he was twelve years old, they went up to the Feast, according to the custom. After the Feast was over, while his parents were returning home, the boy Jesus stayed behind in Jerusalem, but they were unaware of it. Thinking he was in their company, they travelled on for a day. Then they began looking for him among their relatives and friends. When they did not find him, they went back to Jerusalem to look for him. After three days they found him in the temple courts, sitting among the teachers, listening to them and asking them questions. Everyone who heard him was amazed at his understanding and his answers. When his parents saw him, they were astonished. His mother said to him, "Son, why have you treated us like this? Your father and I have been anxiously searching for you." "Why were you searching for me?" he asked. "Didn't you know I had to be in my Father's house?" But they did not understand what he was saying to them. Then he went down to Nazareth with them and was obedient to them. But his mother treasured all these things in her heart. And Jesus grew in wisdom and stature, and in favour with God and men.

1 Outline the event in Jesus' life when he became lost in the temple.
2 The story of Jesus lost in the temple is remembered at Epiphany. Why do you think that it is a suitable story for Epiphany?

Task 3

1 Why do you think that Christians give up things they enjoy during Lent?
2 'I give up cabbage in Lent because I do not like it.' Do you think that this person has understood the reason why Christians give up things in Lent? Explain your answer.

Task 4

The Crucifixion by Andrea Mantegna (1431–1506)

1 On which day in the Church year do Christians remember Jesus' death on a cross?
2 Explain why the death of Jesus is important to Christians.

Task 5

1 a What events in the life of Jesus does an Easter garden represent?
  b Why are these events in the life of Jesus important for Christians?
2 'The Christian faith would not have developed if the tomb had not been empty on Easter morning.' Do you agree? Give reasons for your answer, showing that you have thought about more than one point of view.

Task 6

1 Outline the events of the first Pentecost.
2 Why does this event mark the beginning of the Christian church?
3 Why do Christians believe that it is part of their duty as a Christian to go out and spread the Christian message to others, and baptise them into the faith?

Task 7

Many of the Christian festivals are based on events in the New Testament. Choose one Christian festival and explain how it is based on the New Testament.

Topic 1 — The baptism of Jesus

What is...?

A **rite** is a religious service or ceremony.

A **rite of passage** is a religious service or ceremony that marks a special stage in a person's life.

God's grace is the special power given to people by God to help them do God's will.

What is...?

Baptism is the religious rite that symbolises admission into the Christian Church, by either the sprinkling of water on a person's forehead or a person's total immersion into water. It is a sacrament.

Activity

Look at page 76. What is a sacrament?

Activity

1 Draw the 'road' of life from birth to death.
2 Mark on your road the stages in life that people might consider special.
3 Compare your special stages with those chosen by others in the class.
4 Are there any stages in life that the majority of the class has considered special?

John the Baptist baptised Jesus in the River Jordan before Jesus began to preach his message.

John was telling people to turn away from sin (**to repent**). After people had confessed their sins to John, he baptised them with water. Jesus was baptised by John the Baptist before he began to preach, to show that he was fully dedicating himself to God's work. Before he was taken up to heaven (ascended), Jesus told his followers to

'Therefore go and make disciples of all nations, baptizing them in the name of the Father, and of the Son and of the Holy Spirit, and teaching them to obey everything I have commanded you. And surely I am with you always, to the very end of the age.' (Matthew 28: 19–20)

The majority of Christians believe that they must be baptised to show that they accept Christ into their life and want to follow his example. Most Christian churches teach that baptism is a sacrament.

Joining the Christian Church

Joining the Church is a stage in life that most Christians believe to be special. It is usually marked by a form of baptism.

Some Christians only baptise people who are old enough to understand what it means to accept Jesus as their saviour. When people accept Jesus, they are believed to have received the inner baptism of the Holy Spirit. Then, to show that they are 'born again', an outward baptism with water is performed. This is called a **believer's baptism**. These churches baptise candidates by **total immersion**. The person to be baptised is lowered backwards **under the water**, while the **minister** will say the **words of baptism**. The baptism will be performed in a pool called a **baptistry**. The Baptist Church uses this form of baptism.

A baptistry is a pool used for a believer's baptism

The Orthodox, Roman Catholic, Methodist and Anglican churches perform infant baptism, because they believe it does not matter that the child does not understand what is happening as God's grace is given without any action on the child's part. Through baptism, the child becomes a member of the Christian family and is given the chance to be 'born again' to a new life free from sin. The baptism takes place at a **font**.

A font is a container of holy water used at baptism

The Salvation Army and the **Society of Friends** (Quakers) do not have a service of baptism, because these churches do not believe an outward action is needed. The Salvation Army believes that people find their own way to salvation. The Society of Friends believes that baptism is not necessary to communicate with God.

? Questions

1 Explain **two** reasons why Christians use baptism.
2 **a** Why do most Christians consider baptism a sacrament?
  b Why is water used as the outward sign in baptism?
3 Why do some Christians believe that a believer's baptism is important?
4 Why do some Christians believe that infant baptism is important?
5 Why do members of the Salvation Army and the Society of Friends believe that baptism is unnecessary?
6 'It is wrong to baptise babies as they have no choice.' Do you agree? Give reasons for your answer, showing that you have thought about more than one point of view.

Topic 2

Believer's baptism

Infant dedication

Baptist churches will have a **service of dedication** to bring the child **into the Christian family,** and **to thank God** for the gift of a child. The child is presented to the Christian community and dedicated to Christ. The parents promise to raise the child as a Christian.

A believer's baptism in the Baptist Church

The Baptist Church baptises people as an outward sign that they have willingly turned to Christ.

The water is a symbol that Christ has washed their sins away by his death on the cross. The pool represents Christ's tomb. As the person is immersed in the water, they are dying with sin and as they come out of the water, they are rising to a new life with Christ, and so are 'born again'.

The first part of the service will consist of hymns, Bible-readings and a sermon (talk) by the minister. They will all be linked to the theme of baptism and the need to follow the example of Christ in one's life. The minister will then explain the reasons for baptism and that baptism is the way in which a person becomes united with Christ. Baptism is an act of faith.

Each person to be baptised will come forward and explain why he or she wants to be baptised. This is called a **testimony**. The person will describe how God has worked in his or her life and why he or she wants to be baptised.

Each candidate will give a testimony before baptism

Before the baptism takes place, the minister will ask those to be baptised to confirm that they have repented their sins, and that they believe in Jesus as their saviour. The minister will ask for God's blessing on them. The minister will enter the pool, and will baptise each candidate in turn. As each person is immersed under the water, the minister will say:

'On the profession of your faith in our Lord Jesus Christ, I baptise you in the name of the Father, and of the Son and of the Holy Spirit.'

After every candidate has been baptised, the service will end with a hymn and a final blessing from the minister.

 Activity

Stephanie gave the following testimony before her believer's baptism. Explain in your own words why she wanted to be baptised.

The candidate will be totally immersed in water during the baptism

Stephanie's testimony

I accepted Jesus Christ as my Saviour when I was 8 years old and now I want to follow with a believer's baptism. Jesus Christ is the centre of my life. As a Christian, I do not claim perfection, but strive to live as I should, according to the example of Christ. My relationship with God provides a peace beyond measure in my life. I am only human, but I can do all things through Christ, which strengthens me. I know Jesus Christ is my personal saviour. I want to accept him in my life today. God sent His only Son to be born of a virgin to bear the sins of the world and die on the cross as a sacrifice for the sins I have and will commit. I cannot imagine the suffering Christ experienced as he hung from that cross, a crown of thorns on His head. Jesus died on the cross that day, and was buried. On the third day, He rose again to sit at the right hand of the Father in heaven. I admit that I am a sinner. I repent of my sins, and ask forgiveness. Oh the joy that has come into my life since the Holy Spirit resided in my heart!

 Questions

Describe and explain a believer's baptism in the Baptist Church. You must pay special attention to the words said and what these words mean.

Topic 3

Infant baptism

What is ...?

Godparents are people chosen to speak on the child's behalf at baptism.

The **Roman Catholic Church** and the **Church of England** baptise a baby by sprinkling water on to his or her forehead at a font. A priest performs the service. As the baby is too young, the promises at the baptism are said on the child's behalf by the parents and godparents.

The parents and godparents will make three promises on the child's behalf. These are:

• to turn to Christ
• to repent sin
• to renounce evil.

The parents and godparents will agree to bring the child up in a Christian home and in the Christian faith. They must declare that they believe in the Trinity.

What do you think?

'A priest has the right to refuse to baptise the child of people who never attend church.' Do you agree? Give reasons for your answer, showing that you have thought about more than one point of view.

Infant baptism in the Church of England

The vicar (priest) will begin the service by reminding the parents and godparents that the child will depend on them to be brought up in the Christian faith. The parents and godparents will make the three promises 'to turn to Christ, to repent sin and to renounce evil' on behalf of the child. The vicar will make the sign of the cross on the forehead of the child with the words, 'I sign you with the cross, the sign of Christ. Do not be ashamed to confess the faith of Christ crucified.' The parents and godparents have to vow that they accept the Trinity. The child is baptised by the vicar at the font. As water is poured over the forehead of the child, the vicar will say the child's name and the words, 'I baptise you in the name of the Father, and of the Son, and of the Holy Spirit'. It is usual to give the parents or godparents a lighted candle as a reminder that the child has passed from the darkness of sin into the light of God. The child is welcomed into the Christian family.

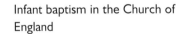

As a class, act out an infant baptism in the Church of England. You will need service sheets, a vicar, the parents and godparents. The rest of the class can form the congregation. You will need to decide if the child is a boy or girl and his or her name. If the child is a boy then he will need two male godparents and one female; if the child is a girl she will need two female godparents and one male.

Baptism in the Roman Catholic Church is very similar to baptism in the Church of England but there are some differences. The Roman Catholic baptism is different because:

- the baptism usually takes place during a Mass so that the whole congregation is present to welcome the child into the Christian family
- the child is anointed with the oil of **catechumens** as a sign of the strength God gives to Christians in the struggle against sin and temptation
- after baptism the child is anointed with oil called **chrism**. This is to consecrate the child to God. It is a sign that the child is being appointed to do important work in God's service
- a white garment is placed around the child to show that through baptism the child has passed from the darkness of sin to the light of Christ.

Infant baptism in the Church of England

1 What are the **three** promises that parents and godparents have to make on behalf of the child?
2 What other promises do the parents and godparents make at the baptism?
3 a Explain how the baptism of a baby in the Roman Catholic Church is similar to baptism in the Church of England.
   b Explain how the baptism of a baby in the Roman Catholic Church is different from baptism in the Church of England.
4 Describe and explain an infant baptism in either the Roman Catholic Church or the Church of England. You must pay special attention to the words used.

Topic 4 Confirmation

What is ...?

Confirmation is the service at which a person who has been baptised becomes a full member of the Christian Church.

In the Roman Catholic Church and the Church of England, confirmation takes place when children are old enough to make the promises made on their behalf at their baptism. Confirmation is a Christian ceremony to mark a person's coming of age as a Christian, as it is when an adult commitment to Christ is made. Candidates for confirmation will be asked to make the promises for themselves that their parents and godparents made on their behalf at their baptism:

- to turn to Christ
- to repent sin
- to renounce evil.

The candidates will be asked if they believe and trust in God the Father, his son Jesus Christ and the Holy Spirit. Confirmation is something **done to** the person not **done by** the person. A bishop performs the service.

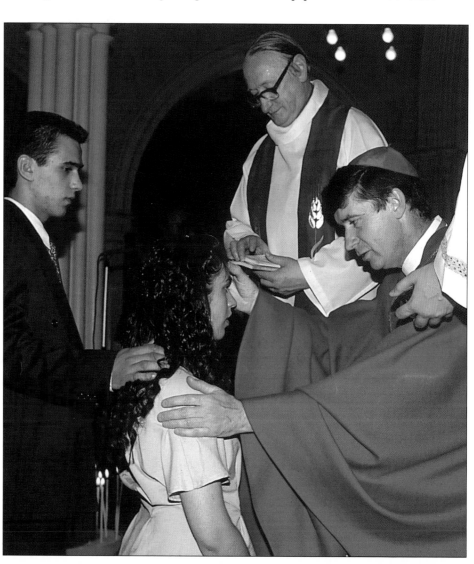

Confirmation is performed by a bishop

The bishop prays as he lays his hands on the candidates' heads, asking God to **confirm** his servants with the Holy Spirit; to make them strong (**firm**) in the faith. The Holy Spirit is asked to strengthen each person's faith and help his or her growth in the faith. The bishop asks that the candidates receive the gifts of the Holy Spirit as they kneel before him.

In the **Roman Catholic Church,** the bishop will place his hand on the candidate's head and say, 'Name, be sealed with the gift of the Holy Spirit'. At the same time, he makes the sign of the cross with the thumb of his right hand. The sign of the cross is made with chrism (oil) on the candidate's forehead. The oil is a symbol of the gifts of the Holy Spirit received at confirmation. The bishop shakes the candidate's hand and says, 'Peace be with you'. The candidate will reply, 'And also with you'.

In the **Church of England** it is unusual to use chrism at a confirmation, or for the bishop to make the sign of the cross. As he places his hands on the candidate's head, the bishop says; 'Confirm, O Lord your servant (name) with the Holy Spirit'.

The service will end with a blessing on those present.

 ## What do you think?

> Look at page 53. Why do you think the fact that the bishop's mitre links with the events of Pentecost is significant at a service of confirmation?

Baptism in the Methodist Church is similar to baptism in the Church of England. The font is a bowl, which is placed on the Communion table during the service. The service takes place in front of the congregation to mark the fact that the child is becoming a member of Christ's family. The baptism will take place during a Sunday morning service.

There is no service of confirmation in the Methodist Church, but teenagers will make a confession of faith in front of the whole congregation to state that they wish to be full members of the church, and to live as Jesus would wish. They are then welcomed as full members of the church by shaking hands with the minister.

Each year at the Covenant service, all Methodists reaffirm their membership of the Church and sign a covenant of belief and intent.

 ## Questions

1 Why do many Christians consider confirmation important?
2 What replaces confirmation in the Methodist Church?
3 Describe a confirmation service in either an Anglican or a Roman Catholic church, paying special attention to the promises that are made. In your answer, explain why confirmation is regarded as important in the denomination that you have chosen.
4 'Confirmation gives people baptised as infants a chance to accept or reject the Christian faith.' Do you agree? Give reasons for your opinion showing that you have thought about more than one point of view.

Topic 5

Baptism in the Orthodox Church

In the **Orthodox Church,** a child becomes a full member of the Church at the time of baptism. This is because the Orthodox Church believes that God's grace is given at baptism without the person making a conscious decision to become a Christian. Baptism is a sign of God's great love. The baptism of babies shows this love as God gives it before one can know or love him. The Church believes that baptism is bearing witness that God has chosen the child to be an important member of His people. From the day of their baptism, children are expected to grow in the life of the Holy Spirit, through their family and the Church.

A child is baptised by total immersion in the Orthodox Church

In the Orthodox Church, the ceremony of baptism begins with prayers asking that the child will come to know God and his commandments. The priest orders Satan to leave the child to show that evil is to be rejected. The child is stripped to show that sin is being removed. The child is turned to the West from which darkness comes. The child is asked if he or she gives up Satan. A sponsor replies on the child's behalf. The child is then turned to the East, the source of light, and asked if Christ is accepted. Again the sponsor replies on behalf of the child. The priest says the Nicene Creed as a reminder of the beliefs the child will be accepting.

The baptism now takes place at a font. The baptismal water is blessed as the sign of the goodness of God's creation. Prayers are said for the child, who is blessed with sanctified oil as the sign that his creation by God is holy and good. The child is totally immersed three times in the water in the name of the Father, the Son and the Holy Spirit. Orthodox Christians believe the immersion is symbolic of the death of sin in the child and the beginning of a new life in Christ.

The child is dried and anointed with olive oil on the hands, feet, ears and mouth in order to dedicate the child to the service of Christ. The child is dressed in new white garments and carried in procession round the font three times.

What do you think?

Why do you think that the child is immersed in the font three times and carried round the font three times?

What is...?

Chrismation is the sacrament of confirmation in the Orthodox Church. It gets its name from the use of chrism oil during the ceremony.

Chrismation follows the baptism. Chrismation, the gift of the Holy Spirit, is performed in the Orthodox Church by anointing all parts of the child's body with **chrism**. In chrismation a person is given the gift of the Holy Spirit from God, in order to live the new life received in baptism. The baby is anointed, just as Christ is the Anointed One of God. It is believed that through chrismation, the child becomes a 'christ', a son of God, a person upon whom the Holy Spirit dwells. This is for as long as the child wants this to happen. Hair is cut from the child's head and shaped into the sign of the cross. Most Orthodox Christians wear this cross for the rest of their lives. The cross is a symbol that the child will offer his or her life to the service of God. The child is now a full member of the church and receives his or her first communion of bread and wine from a spoon.

Questions

1 Describe and explain a baptism in the Orthodox Church, paying special attention to the words used during the service.
2 a Describe the ceremony of chrismation, which follows baptism in the Orthodox Church.
 b Explain the significance of this ceremony for the child.

Topic 6

Christian marriage services

 **What is...?**

Marriage is the legal union between a man and a woman in order to live together and often to have children.

 Activity

1 Find out what the legal requirements are for a couple to get married in England and Wales.
2 List these requirements in your book.

Christians believe that it is important that God blesses their marriage and therefore they usually choose to be married at the place where they regularly worship. Christians agree God established marriage at the time of creation and that couples are to be faithful to their partner for life. However, there are variations between the marriage ceremonies of the different Christian denominations.

 Activity

Using the information that follows, write a detailed account of a marriage ceremony in the Church of England, paying special attention to the words used.

Church of England marriage ceremony

The ceremony begins with a reminder by the vicar (priest) that marriage is an important and serious step and a gift from God. A description of the meaning of the wedding vows and the three reasons why God established marriage follows.

'It is God's purpose that as husband and wife give themselves to each other in love throughout their lives, they shall be united in that love as Christ is united with his Church. Marriage is given, that the husband and wife may comfort and help each other, living faithfully together in need and in plenty, in sorrow and in joy. It is given that with delight and tenderness, they may know each other in love, and through the joy of their bodily union, may strengthen the unions of their hearts and lives. It is given, that they may have children and be blessed in caring for them, and bringing them up in accordance with God's will, to his praise and glory.'

The congregation is asked to pray for the couple and asked if there is any legal reason why the couple may not be married. The couple is then asked the same question. The nature of the relationship between a husband and wife is established as they exchange their vows. The vicar will ask the bride and groom in turn if:

'(Name), will you take (Name) to be your husband/wife? Will you love him/her, comfort him/her, honour and protect him/her, and forsaking all others, be faithful to him/her as long as you both shall live?'

The bride and groom will agree that:

'I, (Name) take you (Name), to be my wife/husband;

to have and to hold; from this day forward;

for better, for worse, for richer, for poorer,

in sickness and in health, to love, and to cherish,

till death us do part, according to God's holy law; and this is my solemn vow.'

Christians believe marriage is for life. This is symbolised by the ring(s) exchanged during the marriage ceremony. The bridegroom places the ring on the fourth finger of the bride's left hand, and holding it there, says:

'I give you this ring as a sign of our marriage. With my body I honour

you, all that I am I give to you, and all that I have I share with you,

within the love of God the Father, Son and Holy Spirit.'

The bridegroom may also receive a ring. The ring is a symbol of the binding relationship into which the couple are entering. The priest declares that they are husband and wife, and only God may end this relationship:

'I therefore proclaim that they are husband and wife. That which God has joined together, let not man divide.'

The ceremony ends with a blessing. There will be hymns, prayers and a talk (sermon) throughout the ceremony, all related to the Christian beliefs about marriage.

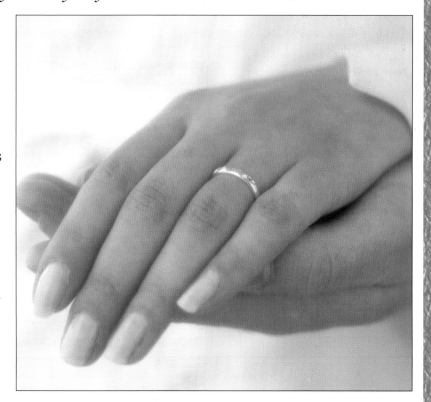

The bride accepts a ring from the bridegroom

The Roman Catholic marriage ceremony

In the Roman Catholic Church, the marriage ceremony is similar to the service in the Church of England but may include a **Nuptial Mass**. In this case, the wedding ceremony takes place after the Liturgy of the Word (readings and prayers) and before the Eucharist service. The first act of the couple's married life, therefore, is to take Communion together to show that their marriage has been blessed by God.

Activity

Look at page 76. What is a Mass?

The Orthodox Church marriage ceremony

A 'crowning' forms part of an Orthodox marriage ceremony

In an Orthodox wedding, the rings are blessed and exchanged at the back of the church. Then the couple move into the church, where the marriage takes place at a table in the centre. Readings from the Bible explain the meaning and purpose of marriage, and the couple hold candles as a symbol of the 'light' or guidance Christians receive from God's Word.

In the Orthodox Church the newly married couple are led round the church three times

The priest then places crowns or circlets of flowers and leaves on the heads of the couple. As he crowns them, the priest will say, 'O Lord God, crown them with glory and honour'. The bride and bridegroom are to be the 'king' and 'queen' of a new family. In the Russian Orthodox Church, the service itself is called **crowning**. The groom is given a crown bearing the image of Christ and the bride's crown has an image of the Virgin Mary. The couple will drink from a chalice of wine because the shared cup is a sign of the life they will now share.

Finally, holding hands, the priest leads the couple in a circle round the centre table, three times as a reminder of the Trinity. A circle is a symbol of the eternal (unending) love of God and thus also a symbol of the couple's hope for an 'unending' marriage.

1 Draw each of the symbols found in an Orthodox marriage ceremony.
2 By the side of each symbol, explain how the symbol represents an aspect of marriage as understood by the Orthodox Church.

Free churches

In the **Methodist** and **Baptist** churches, the service will be similar to that of the Church of England, with vows, Bible-readings, hymns, prayers and a sermon. However, the words may vary from ceremony to ceremony. The couple may exchange a ring but these denominations do not believe that a ring is necessary to symbolise that marriage is for life.

The Society of Friends (Quakers) performs a marriage service during the meeting for Worship. The couple stand, join hands and declare that they take the other as husband/wife and will be faithful for life.

'Friends, I take this my Friend (name) to be my wife/husband, promising through divine assistance to be unto her/him a loving and faithful husband/wife as long as we both on Earth shall live.'

Look at page 89. What happens at a Quaker Worship meeting?

Some Christian couples are unable to marry in church but may still wish to make vows to each other during their marriage ceremony. Write a set of marriage vows for them.

'Marriage is an outdated practice.' Do you agree? Give reasons for your answer, showing that you have thought about more than one point of view.

1 In the Church of England, what vows do the bride and bridegroom make to each other before the ring is placed on the bride's finger?
2 What does the ring represent?
3 a What is a Nuptial Mass?
  b Why do you think that many couples in the Roman Catholic Church choose to start married life with a Nuptial Mass?
4 a What is a 'crowning' in an Orthodox marriage ceremony?
  b What is the significance of a 'crowning'?
5 'A simple Quaker marriage ceremony has more meaning for the couple than the ceremonies of the other Christian denominations.' Do you agree? Give reasons for your opinion showing that you have thought about more than one point of view.

Topic 7

Christian funerals

What is ...?

A **funeral** is the ceremony of burial or cremation of a dead person.

A **committal** involves the burial of the body in a cemetery after a funeral service.

A **cremation** involves the burning of the body at a crematorium after a funeral service.

The **deceased** is the term used to describe the person who has died.

Christians believe that life continues after death. Christians often talk about heaven and hell as the place to which people go after death. Christians are not in agreement as to what heaven and hell are like but there is general agreement that heaven is to be with God and hell is for those who are lost to God.

What do you think?

What do you think happens to people after death? Discuss your ideas with your teacher and the rest of your class.

Christian funerals are influenced by the faith's beliefs about life after death. Christians have confidence that if people have followed Jesus' example the deceased will be with God in heaven and they will meet again after death. However, Christians recognise that like any parting from a loved one, a funeral is a sad time.

As a funeral marks the end of a person's life, then it is appropriate to have a ceremony, which offers people the opportunity to pay their respects to the person who has died, pay tribute to his or her good qualities and express thankfulness for the person's life. Funerals help the family and friends of the dead person to express their grief and to say good-bye. Traditional funeral wreaths are circles made from evergreens to symbolise the Christian belief that death is not the end and that there is life after death.

The family of the deceased has to choose whether the dead person is to be buried (a **committal**) or **cremated**. The funeral service is similar for either type of funeral. There may be a church service before the service at the graveside or at the crematorium.

A Christian funeral in a Methodist church

The minister uses the words of Jesus as the coffin is carried to the front of the church. 'I am the resurrection and the life. He who believes in me will live, even though he dies; and whoever lives and believes in me will never die' (John 11: 25–26). The minister is reminding the congregation that the dead person, as a Christian, believed in life after death.

After a prayer, a hymn is sung. Hymns, such as 'Abide with me', will remind people of the Christian hope of life after death. The hymn will be followed by a Bible-reading on the same theme. The minister will give a brief talk about the person who has died. This talk is called a **eulogy** and stresses the dead person's good qualities. A prayer asking for comfort for the person's family and friends follows a prayer thanking God for the life of the deceased. Another hymn is sung. It could be Psalm 23 or 'The Day thou gavest Lord is ended'. It may be the deceased's favourite hymn. The service ends with a blessing for the dead person's soul and for the bereaved (the family and friends).

The second part of the service may be in a cemetery or in a crematorium. As the coffin is lowered into the grave or removed from view, the minister says, 'We entrust our brother/sister to God's merciful keeping and we now commit his/her body to the ground. Earth to earth, ashes to ashes, dust to dust; in sure and certain hope of the resurrection to eternal life through our Lord Jesus Christ, who died, was buried and rose again for us. To Him be the glory for ever and ever. Amen.'

The funeral has ended on a note of hope rather than despair, expressing the strong Christian belief that death is not the end. It is the beginning of eternal or everlasting life.

A **committal** involves the burial of the body in a cemetery after a funeral service

 Activity

A eulogy is a brief talk about the person who has died. Choose a famous person, living or dead, that you admire. Write a suitable eulogy for his or her funeral service.

Why do you think that the following verse from Psalm 23 is considered appropriate for a funeral service?

> *The Lord is my shepherd, I shall not be in want.*
>
> *He makes me lie down in green pastures,*
>
> *he leads me beside quiet waters, he restores my soul.*
>
> *He guides me in paths of righteousness for his name's sake.*
>
> *Even though I walk through the valley of the shadow of death,*
>
> *I will fear no evil, for you are with me; your rod and your staff, they comfort me. ...*

In most Christian denominations, the funeral service is similar to the Methodist one described above. A Roman Catholic funeral may include a Requiem Mass as part of the service. God is thanked for the life of the dead person and His forgiveness is asked for any sins the person may have committed in life. The service in the Orthodox Church, however, is different from other Christian denominations in both the format and the symbols used.

The Orthodox funeral service

The body is washed and put in new clothes before the funeral service. This is an outward sign of the new life the person is beginning. A strip of material containing the pictures of Jesus, the Virgin Mary and John the Baptist is placed on the forehead. This represents the victory wreath of an athlete who has successfully run his race. A picture of Jesus is placed in the hands of the deceased as a sign that the person believed in Jesus and gave his life to him. Then the body is covered with a special cloth as a sign of the protection given by Jesus.

At the funeral, four candlesticks are placed at the sides of the coffin to form a cross. The mourners hold lighted candles as a sign that the dead person's life has not been extinguished. During the Orthodox service, everyone present is made to face up to the basic questions of life and death. The deceased lies in the centre of the church facing the altar. The coffin is open so that the body is in full view. Everyone present is reminded that death will happen and to be prepared for it. The prayers and Bible-readings emphasise eternal life and the resurrection of Christ. The church is full of lights. The priest wears white vestments. The funeral is regarded as a time of celebration as the person will have risen to be with Christ.

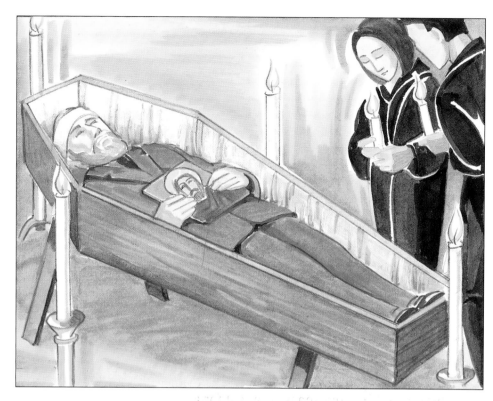

At an Orthodox funeral the coffin is open

Activity

Write out each of the symbols used in an Orthodox funeral service. Explain what each symbol means and how it links to the Christian ideas about life and death.

What do you think?

'When you are dead, you are dead so a funeral is not really important.' Do you agree? Give reasons for your answer, showing that you have thought about more than one point of view.

Questions

1 a Explain what Christians believe about life after death.
 b How do their beliefs about life after death and the resurrection of the body influence Christians' attitudes towards funerals?
2 Choose one Christian denomination and describe its funeral service. In your account pay particular attention to the words used.
3 Why do you think many Roman Catholic funerals include a Requiem Mass?
4 What is the difference between a committal and a cremation?
5 'A Christian funeral is a sad occasion.' Do you agree? Give reasons for your opinion, showing that you have thought about more than one point of view.

Do you understand...

the Christian rites of baptism, marriage and funerals

Task 1

A baptistry

1 a Name a denomination in which a pool like the one in the picture is used for baptism.
   b Why does this denomination believe in the baptism of adults?
2 What might the person who is to be baptised say before the baptism?
3 What promises will the person make before the baptism?
4 a What does the pool represent?
   b Why is baptism performed by total immersion in this denomination?

A font

Task 2

1 How is a font used?
2 What promises do the parents and godparents make during the service of baptism?
3 What responsibilities do the parents and godparents accept?
4 What words does the priest say as he baptises the child?
5 Why do many Christians believe that it is important to baptise infants?
6 'It is better to be baptised when you can make your own choice to become a full member of the Christian faith.'
   Do you agree? Give reasons for your answer, showing that you have thought about more than one point of view.

Task 3

1 In the picture, the bishop has a crozier (held by his assistant). What does a crozier represent?
2 How are baptism and confirmation linked?
3 **a** Describe a confirmation service in either an Anglican or a Roman Catholic church, paying special attention to the promises that are made.
   b Explain why confirmation is regarded as important in the denomination you have chosen.
4 'Confirmation is not needed to make a Christian a full member of the Church.' Do you agree? Give reasons for your answer, showing you have thought about more than one point of view.

Confirmation is performed by a bishop

Task 4

1 Write down and explain the **three** reasons for marriage stated at the beginning of the Church of England wedding ceremony.
2 State and explain the promises the bride and the bridegroom make to each other during the ceremony.
3 Why do many couples exchange a ring in Christian marriage ceremonies?
4 'If a couple do not attend church regularly then the vicar should have the right to refuse to marry them'? Do you agree? Give reasons for your answer, showing that you have thought about more than one point of view.

Many graves are marked with a gravestone

Task 5

1 Why do you think that John Smith's gravestone has a cross on it?
2 Why is a cross an important symbol for Christians?
3 **a** Describe a funeral service in **one** Christian denomination.
   b What is the importance of a funeral service for a Christian?
4 'Heaven exists and is a beautiful place.' Do you think a belief in heaven would be a comfort to a Christian at a funeral? Give reasons for your answer, showing that you have thought about more than one point of view.

Sacramental worship

Activity

Look at pages 80 and 86. What is the difference between liturgical and non-liturgical worship?

What is...?

Consecration is to make or declare something dedicated to God.

Public worship is worship that is open to, or shared with, other Christians

Sacramental worship happens when it is believed that in the service there is an outward sign of an inward gift from God.

The rite of baptism in most Christian denominations is regarded as a sacrament. Another form of sacramental worship is the service of Holy Communion. The majority of Christians celebrate Holy Communion to re-enact the words and actions of Jesus at the Last Supper on Maundy Thursday. Christians celebrate Holy Communion to remember Jesus' death on the cross, which they believe saved the world from the punishment deserved from God for sin.

Activity

Imagine that you were one of the guests at the Last Supper. Write a letter to a friend telling them what happened at the meal. Include in your letter the actual words and actions of Jesus at the Last Supper. To help you write your letter look at Mark's account of the Last Supper on page 46.

Holy Communion

Christian denominations use several names to describe the service of Holy Communion. The name chosen by a particular denomination is linked to its understanding of the significance of the bread and wine during the service.

The **Roman Catholic Church** calls the service of Holy Communion, the **Mass**. This name comes from the words at the end of the Latin service and refers to the sending out of the worshippers to serve Christ in their daily life. The **Orthodox Church** calls the service the **Divine Liturgy** because it has a set order established by God. The Roman Catholic and Orthodox Christians believe that when the priest consecrates the bread and wine, the bread and wine become the actual body and blood of Christ. These Christians believe that Christ's sacrifice for the forgiveness of sins is repeated at each service of Holy Communion. The bread and wine are believed to be food and drink for the spiritual life of the communicants (ie those taking part in the Mass), to gain eternal life and God's forgiveness.

The **Church of England** calls the service of Holy Communion the **Eucharist**. Eucharist means '**thanksgiving**' and, at the central point of the service, the congregation gives thanks to God for all his gifts in creation, and for all that he has done through Jesus Christ. The Church of England believes that the spirit of Christ is present in the bread and wine, but the bread and wine do not change into the body and blood of Christ. They believe that when they take the bread and wine, they join with Christ and his spirit enters them alongside the bread and wine.

The **Free churches** who accept Holy Communion tend to use the simplest name for the service such as the **Lord's Supper**, or the **Breaking of Bread**. The names recall the fellowship between Jesus and his disciples at the Last Supper. Jesus was host to the disciples at the Last Supper and the worshippers believe that when they hold the service of Holy Communion, they are the guests of Jesus at the Lord's Supper. In these forms of the service of Holy Communion, the emphasis is on the shared meal and a memorial in remembrance of Christ's sacrifice. These Christian denominations believe that it is through remembrance of Christ's death that the Christian faith is strengthened, and that by sharing a meal Christian fellowship is shown. The majority of Free churches accept this understanding of Holy Communion.

The Salvation Army and **the Society of Friends** (Quakers) do not celebrate Holy Communion. They believe that communion with God is an inward grace brought through the gift of the Holy Spirit and no outward action is needed. These denominations believe that God's love, mercy and forgiveness are not confined to special times, and believe that every meal should be regarded as a reminder of the Last Supper because Jesus is always present in the hearts of the believers.

? Questions

1 What is the meaning of the word 'Eucharist'?
2 Give **four** other names by which the Eucharist is known.
3 What was the original meal on which the service of Holy Communion is based?
4 What do Roman Catholic and Orthodox Christians believe happens to the bread and wine when the priest speaks the Eucharist prayers over them?
5 What do Roman Catholic and Orthodox Christians believe happens to those who receive the consecrated bread and wine?
6 Many Free churches believe that the service is a memorial.
   a What is a 'memorial'?
   b Why do many Christians believe that the bread and wine should be taken at a service if it is only a memorial?
7 Explain why the Salvation Army and the Society of Friends do not celebrate Holy Communion.

Topic 2 Forms of Holy Communion

The Roman Catholic Mass

The Roman Catholic Church teaches that the Mass is the most important act of worship. Roman Catholics are taught to attend Mass every Sunday, on certain important feast days and as often thereafter as possible. There are important features to a Mass.

As the worshippers enter the church they dip their fingers in the **stoup** (ie a container of holy water) and make the sign of the cross. Roman Catholics believe that only an ordained priest may bless the bread and wine. When the priest consecrates the bread and wine, through the action of the Holy Spirit, the bread and wine become the actual body and blood of Christ. This is called **transubstantiation**. Roman Catholics believe that Christ is present and his sacrifice is repeated at each Mass. Christ's presence means the congregation must show respect, and this involves bowing from the knee and the use of incense. Throughout the service, the congregation will make set responses to the words used by the priest.

 ### What do you think?

The service follows the order set out in the Missal or Mass book. Look at page 80. What name is given to services with a set pattern or form?

The Mass begins with the **Greeting of the People** by the priest and prayers asking God to forgive sins. This is followed by the **Liturgy of the Word**. The priest reads passages from the Bible suitable to the time of year or for the specific Mass. After the Gospel reading the priest will make the sign of the cross and swing the censer (incense-burner) over the book. A sermon follows and a statement of belief called the Nicene Creed. Five prayers for the Faithful follow.

The **Liturgy of the Eucharist**, the most important part of the service, now takes place. The bread, wine, and collections are brought to the altar. The bread is placed on a dish called a **paten**. The wine is held in a cup called a **chalice**. The priest prays that the gifts are acceptable to God, and swings the incense over them. The priest washes his hands and the congregation prays. The priest thanks and praises God, and asks the Holy Spirit to make the bread and wine holy. A bell rings to welcome the Holy Spirit. The priest spreads his hands over them and as he prays, he uses the words of Jesus at the Last Supper. The priest consecrates the bread and wine. As he does this, he lifts the bread and then the wine for the congregation to see. The

The central part of the Mass takes place at an altar

bread and wine are now called the **Host,** and the raising of the bread and wine by the priest is called the **Elevation of the Host.** As this happens, a bell is rung three times. This is the moment when transubstantiation takes place. The congregation shows adoration in silence. The priest reminds them of the meaning of Christ's sacrifice for their sins, and that by taking communion the congregation share in this sacrifice. There are further prayers and the **sign of peace** is offered, when the congregation shakes hands with each other.

The bread used in the Roman Catholic Church is called the **wafer.** The priest holds up a wafer and breaks it in half to symbolise how Christ's body was broken on the cross. The priest will now eat the wafer and drink the wine. The congregation come forward and stand in line to receive the wafer, which the priest places on their tongues, saying, 'The body of Christ'. If the wine is given he says, 'The blood of Christ'.

The service ends with a blessing from the priest and the words 'The Mass is ended. Go in peace to love and serve the Lord.' Roman Catholics are being reminded that because of Jesus' sacrifice for their sins, it is part of their duty as believers to work for others.

❓ Questions

1 What do Roman Catholics believe happens to the bread and wine when the priest consecrates them?
2 Why do you think that the Mass is believed to be the most important service in the Roman Catholic Church?
3 Describe a Roman Catholic Mass, paying particular attention to the words used.

The Church of England Holy Communion

In the Church of England, Holy Communion may only be celebrated by an **ordained** bishop or priest, who will always perform four acts in the service. These are:

- taking the bread and wine
- giving thanks over them, using Jesus' words at the Last Supper
- breaking the bread
- distributing the bread and wine to those people taking Holy Communion (the **communicants**).

The service is a **liturgy** as it follows the service set down in either the Book of Common Prayer or the Alternative Service Book. The service is similar to the Roman Catholic Mass, except that it is unusual for incense to be used, and in the Church of England service the congregation come forward and kneel in front of the altar as they receive the bread and wine.

The service begins with **The Liturgy of the Word**, which concentrates on **teaching** the faith by readings from the Bible, including a passage from one of the Gospels. Normally there is a sermon. The congregation recite the Nicene Creed and make a joint confession of their sins:

Eleven per cent of the population of England attend church regularly on Sunday

'Almighty God, our heavenly Father, we have sinned against you and against our fellow men, in thought and word and deed, through negligence, through weakness, through our own deliberate fault. We are truly sorry and repent of all our sins.'

The vicar (priest) assures them of God's forgiveness, and prayers of intercession for all the concerns of the Church and the world, for fellow Christians, especially the bishop, for peace among nations and for those in need, follow. People known to the congregation who are sick or troubled may be prayed for by name. Those who have recently died in the parish will be remembered.

The Liturgy of the Sacrament is the central part of the service and begins with the exchange of Peace. The vicar exchanges a spoken greeting with the congregation, and members of the congregation turn and greet each other in friendship and as a demonstration of Christ's love, which should be present among Christians. The Book of Common Prayer says, 'It is essential that those who take Holy Communion are in love and charity with their neighbours'. The bread and wine are placed on the altar, and a collection may be taken of the people's offerings of money for the work of the church. The vicar gives thanks to God for his gifts and especially for

What do you think?

'You can be a Christian without attending church.' Do you agree? Give reasons for your answer, showing that you have thought about more than one point of view.

the gift of His Son. Jesus' own words at the Last Supper are used as the vicar prays for the coming of the Holy Spirit.

The following extract from the Alternative Service Book describes the words and actions of the vicar as the bread and wine is consecrated:

> Who in the same night that he was betrayed, (Here the priest is to take the Paten into his hands), took bread; and gave you thanks; (And here the priest breaks the bread), he broke it, and gave it to his disciples, saying, 'Take, eat, (And here to lay his hand upon the bread), this is my Body, which is given for you; do this in remembrance of me'. Likewise, after supper, he took the cup; (Here he is to take the Cup into his hands), and gave you thanks, he gave it to them, saying, 'Drink this all of you; (And here he lays his hand on the chalice containing the wine), this is my blood of the new covenant, which is shed for you, and for many, for the forgiveness of sins; Do this, as often as you drink it, in remembrance of me.' It is a very holy moment as the congregation joins silently in the prayer before the priest invites them to take the bread and wine. The priest and congregation will say the prayer Jesus taught us: 'Our Father...'.

The congregation will receive the bread and wine as they kneel before the altar. As the wafer (bread) is given, the priest will say, '**The body of Christ keep you in eternal life**'. As people receive the wine from the chalice, the priest will say, '**The blood of Christ keep you in eternal life**'.

The service ends with prayers of thankfulness, a commitment to living the Christian way of life in the world, a blessing and the dismissal.

⑦ Questions

1 Who can celebrate the service of Holy Communion in the Church of England?
2 Which **four** acts are always included in the service of Holy Communion?
3 The service begins with the Liturgy of the Word.
   a On what does this section of the service concentrate?
   b What may be included in this section of the service?
4 Describe in detail the Liturgy of the Sacrament in the Church of England, paying particular attention to the words and actions of the priest.

6: Christian forms of worship

What do you think?

Why do you think that the Orthodox Church calls the service of Holy Communion the Divine Liturgy?

The Orthodox Church's Divine Liturgy

In the Orthodox Church, the priest prepares the bread and the wine in the **Chapel of Preparation**. The congregation will hand the priest a list of names and the bread that they have baked. Each person on the list will be especially remembered during the service, and a small piece of bread will be cut for him or her, and placed with the loaf to be consecrated. This means that those named will be brought before God's throne. Prayers will be sung as the bread is prepared.

The Liturgy begins when the priest comes among the people with incense. Prayers, Bible-readings and a sermon follow. This will be followed by a procession led by the priest carrying the bread and wine in the holy vessels. Servers follow with candles and incense. The congregation bow as the procession passes through them. The procession passes behind a screen called the **iconostasis**. This screen is covered with pictures of Jesus, Mary and saints. These pictures are called icons. In the centre of the screen are double doors called the **Royal Doors**. During the service, these doors are opened and closed. The procession passes through the doors and places the bread and wine on the altar, which is called the **Holy Throne**. The doors are now closed to symbolise that the gifts have been taken by God to be changed and given back to the world. The doors will then be re-opened. The congregation is able to see little of what is happening behind the screen. This is symbolic of the fact that the Liturgy is a mystery from God of which humankind sees only part. The congregation comes closer to heaven through the Liturgy. The screen shows that man is separated from God, who is in Heaven, and it is only through Christ's death that God comes within man's reach.

What do you think?

The doors in the centre of the screen are called the Royal Doors and the altar is called the Holy Throne. Why do you think Orthodox Christians have chosen to describe these features in this way?

The congregation give each other the kiss of peace and further prayers are said. The priest now uses the words of Jesus at the Last Supper. The Prayer of Consecration asks the Holy Spirit to come into the bread and wine. Further prayers, including the Lord's Prayer and a hymn to the Blessed Virgin, are said. The priest now raises the consecrated bread for all to see. The choir sings and bells ring. The Holy Spirit has descended into the bread and wine and changed them into the body and blood of Christ. The priest comes to stand at the top of the steps in front of the Royal Doors. The congregation come forward in a line to receive communion. The bread is placed in the wine and given to the congregation from a **spoon**.

The service ends with thanksgiving, a blessing and the service of **Antidoron**, when everyone present comes forward, kisses the cross that is held by the priest and receives a small piece of bread called the antidoron. This sharing of bread is a sign of fellowship and love. This action is a reminder of the Love Feasts which the early Christians shared.

The congregation receive the bread and wine on a spoon

 Activity

1 Divide a piece of paper into **three** columns.
2 Label one column the Church of England, one column the Roman Catholic Church and the third column the Orthodox Church.
3 Under each heading, list the different features of that Church's service of Holy Communion.
4 Compare the similarities and differences between the three denominations.

 Questions

1 The Orthodox Church believes that transubstantiation takes place when the priest consecrates the bread and wine. What do the Christians in this denomination believe happens to the bread and wine at this time?
2 Why do you think that the Orthodox service ends with the service of Antidoron?
3 Describe a Divine Liturgy, paying particular attention to the symbolic actions throughout the service.

6: Christian forms of worship

The Roman Catholic Church, Church of England and Orthodox Church perform the Liturgy of the Word at an altar because an altar is a place of sacrifice and these churches believe that in some way Christ's sacrifice for sin is repeated during the Eucharist. These churches believe that the consecrated bread must be treated with respect. The consecrated bread and wine will be kept in a special safe called a **tabernacle** or **aumbry**. When this safe contains consecrated bread and wine, a light will burn outside it to show the presence of Jesus. The priest will take the consecrated bread and wine with him when he visits the sick and dying, so that they can receive Holy Communion at home.

The consecrated bread and wine is kept in a tabernacle close to the altar

Free churches

Free churches that celebrate Holy Communion do not believe that Christ is present in the bread and wine. These denominations see the service as a remembrance of the Last Supper. People who are not ordained serve the bread and wine, as it is not believed that the bread and wine change in any way. The service symbolises a shared meal to strengthen faith, and therefore a table is used instead of an altar. Individual pieces of bread and glasses of wine are distributed to the congregation so that they are able to eat the bread and drink the wine together to stress the idea of sharing.

The Roman Catholic Church, Church of England and Orthodox Church use alcoholic wine during the service of Holy Communion, as they believe that Jesus would have blessed alcoholic wine at the Last Supper, and they want to make a direct link with the Last Supper. Most Free churches use non-alcoholic wine because alcohol is seen as a cause of many of the evils of modern society.

The Roman Catholic Church and the Church of England use **unleavened** bread (bread without yeast) because the Last Supper was a Passover meal, and Jews use unleavened bread at this meal. The Orthodox Church and Free churches use bread made with yeast. They believe that by using the bread they regularly eat, they show that Holy Communion is not outdated but a reality for today. By sharing a loaf, the unity of the believers in the one Body of Christ is symbolised.

 Activity

1 Divide into small groups of at least five.
2 Imagine that the group is taking part in a religious programme on Radio 4, in which the importance of Holy Communion is under discussion.
3 As a group, act out the discussion.
4 Each member of the group needs to take the part of a Christian who will have a view on the sacrament of Holy Communion, such as a Roman Catholic priest, a vicar in the Church of England, a Baptist and a Quaker. You will also need one member of the group to act as chairperson to keep the discussion in order.

Non-sacramental worship

Services that are not believed to contain an outward sign of an inner gift from God are called **non-sacramental**. Forms of non-sacramental worship are held in **all** Christian churches. In the Roman Catholic Church, Church of England and Orthodox Church these services are still liturgies because they follow a set order in a prayer book. In the Free churches, the order of service varies from week to week, and the services are spontaneous.

 What do you think?

'It is better to follow a set pattern so that you know what to expect when you go to church.' Do you agree? Give reasons for your answer, showing that you have thought about more than one point of view.

 Questions

1 What is a tabernacle used for?
2 a Why do some churches use unleavened bread during the service of Holy Communion?
  b Why do other churches use bread made from yeast in the service?
3 a Why do some churches use alcoholic wine during the service of Holy Communion?
  b Why do other churches believe it is wrong to use alcoholic wine in the service?
4 Explain how the celebration of Holy Communion in the Free churches is different from a Roman Catholic Mass.

Topic 3 Non-sacramental worship

Charismatic
means 'gift' and
Charismatic
Christians are
Christians who
believe that it is
possible to receive
the gifts of the
Holy Spirit. The
gifts of the Holy
Spirit include the
gift of prophecy,
the gift of healing,
the gift to perform
miracles and the
gift of preaching.

Worship in Free churches

A typical service in a Free church, such as the Baptist Church, will consist of hymns and prayers. The most important part of any service in a Free church is the preaching of God's word. Central to the worship are the Bible-readings and the sermon. These churches believe that listening to God's word and putting it into practice is the way to avoid sin and to achieve eternal life with God.

Church choirs

Hymns form an important part of worship in many churches as they not only praise God, but remind the congregation of the Christian message through their words. The music expresses emotions, such as joy and sorrow, and this can help Christians show their feelings about the Christian festival or ceremony. Many churches have choirs to lead the worship. This is to make sure that God is praised in the best way possible. Choirs will often perform special pieces of music, such as Handel's 'Messiah', as additional praise of God and to help people understand the Christian message.

The Pentecostal Church

Pentecostalists believe that the gifts of the Holy Spirit are still available to the faithful. As the denomination's worship concentrates on the gifts of the Holy Spirit, it is linked to the Charismatic tradition in Christianity. A minister or pastor leads the service. A Pentecostal service is very lively, with the congregation clapping and dancing. It is not **liturgical worship**, as it does not have a fixed form or order and the worship is spontaneous. Songs and hymns are often based exactly on the words from the Bible. Worshippers raise their hands in the air as they praise and thank God for everything done for them. When worshippers agree with what someone has said, there are cries of 'Alleluia' and 'Amen'. Sometimes members of the congregation seem overwhelmed by God's Holy Spirit and they almost faint and fall to the floor. Other worshippers believe that they have the gift of prophecy and can 'hear' God's voice and say what it means. Many 'speak in tongues', **glossolalia**, as they feel so moved by the Holy Spirit that normal speech seems inadequate. To outsiders it sounds like a jumble of sounds, but other members of the Church appear to understand what is being said and translate the sounds for the rest of the congregation. At some services, people are cured of illnesses through their faith (faith healing).

Pentecostal worship is very lively

The House Church movement

This is the most recent Christian denomination to develop. The House Church seeks the same gifts from the Holy Spirit as the Pentecostalists. Members of this denomination believe that they are re-creating the worship of the Early Church. Worship takes place in members' homes, in groups of fourteen. Everyone has a role in the worship. The group sits in a circle to show that everyone is equal. A Sunday morning act of worship will have hymns, prayers, Bible-readings and the passing round of bread and wine. There will be an evening service, which may consist of readings from the New Testament. There will be a weekday service, when the readings will be taken from the Old Testament. The aim of the group is to learn to live their lives according to the Bible, which they believe is the direct word of God.

? **Questions**

1 Why do many churches have choirs to lead the singing?
2 Why is hymn-singing an important part of worship in many churches?
3 **a** Why has the Pentecostal Church chosen this name?
   b What is 'speaking in tongues'?
   c Describe a typical Pentecostal service.
4 **a** Where does the House Church denomination worship?
   b Describe a typical Sunday morning worship in this denomination.
   c How do Sunday evening and weekday meetings differ from each other in this denomination?

The Salvation Army

Worship in the Salvation Army is based on the idea that by avoiding sin and following Jesus everyone can be saved and go to heaven. If this is to happen then good must conquer evil. The Salvation Army believe that they are an army fighting the evils of the world in God's cause. The members wear uniforms and have army ranks. The Army see it as their duty to worship God not only in a building but also by helping the less-fortunate members of society. The work of the Salvation Army includes:

- providing hostels for the homeless
- taking soup out to those sleeping rough on the streets
- organising a service to trace missing persons
- helping unmarried mothers, alcoholics and anyone else in need
- touring public houses selling the 'War Cry' paper and trying to warn people of the evils of alcohol.

The place of worship of the Salvation Army is called a **citadel**. Bible-reading is the most important part of the worship, as it is regarded as the way to come closer to God. In the Worship Hall there is a raised platform in front of which there is the **Holiness table**. There will be a large open Bible on this table as a sign that people draw nearer to God by hearing God's word.

The Sunday morning service is called the **Holiness meeting** and it is aimed at teaching Christians how to lead a better life. The evening service is called the **Salvation meeting** and is aimed at bringing non-Christians to God. There is no set pattern to the worship and the leader of the service plans the order of each service. Anyone may lead the service, although an officer usually leads it. Personal testimonies are often made during the service. People come forward to confess their sins while sitting on the **Mercy** seat, a wooden bench at the front of the hall. The person will ask God for forgiveness and to be saved. Other people may sit in the seat and describe how God has helped them to lead better lives. Music is an important part of the worship and the Salvation Army will accompany the hymn-singing.

An officer usually leads worship in the Salvation Army

Activity

Design a leaflet to be handed out in the street by members of the Salvation Army to explain the work of the Army and why the work is important. Include in your leaflet a description of a Salvation meeting, and an invitation for people to attend.

The Society of Friends (Quakers)

Members of the Society of Friends are also called Quakers. The denomination has no formal services, and they do not include hymn-singing. Quakers sit quietly meditating until someone feels moved by the Holy Spirit to speak. When a Quaker stands to speak this is called a ministry. A meeting lasts for an hour without anyone speaking, or several people may speak in turn and share their thoughts with the meeting. Someone might say a prayer, or read a section of the Bible or a poem. At the end of the hour, one of the leaders of the group will bring the service to a close by shaking hands with the person each side of them. At the end of the service, notices are read.

The Society of Friends sit in a circle for worship

Activity

Imagine you are a Quaker and write a letter to a friend who is not a member of your denomination. Include in your letter a description of the worship in a Quaker Meeting. Explain how worship in your denomination is different from worship in other Christian denominations.

Questions

1 Why does the Salvation Army believe that it is an army?
2 Describe a Holiness meeting in the Salvation Army.
3 What is a ministry in a Quaker service?
4 'The Salvation Army worships God in the street as well as in the citadel.' Do you agree? Give reasons for your answer, showing you have thought about more than one point of view.

Do you understand...
Christian worship?

Task 1

1 What did Jesus say at the Last Supper as he gave the disciples the bread and the wine?
2 Christians understand the words of Jesus in different ways. State the different ways in which Christians might understand the words of Jesus at the Last Supper.
3 a Why do some churches hold the service of Holy Communion at an altar?
   b Why do other churches use a table?
4 a Why do some churches use unleavened bread for Holy Communion?
   b Why do other churches use bread made from yeast?
5 a Why do some churches use alcoholic wine for Holy Communion?
   b Why do other churches use non-alcoholic wine?
6 a Name two denominations which do not celebrate the service of Holy Communion.
   b Explain why these churches do not celebrate the service.

A service of Holy Communion

Task 2

1 In which Christian denomination is this service of Holy Communion taking place?
2 What does this denomination believe happens to the bread and wine during the service?
3 Describe the service of Holy Communion in this denomination, paying particular attention to the words used.
4 How is the service of Holy Communion in this Christian denomination different from the Mass in the Roman Catholic Church?
5 a Why is Holy Communion an important part of the worship for many Christians?
   b Why do other denominations consider taking the bread and wine to be of lesser importance to hearing the word of God?

Task 3

> Onward Christian soldiers!
> Marching as to war,
> With the cross of Jesus
> Going on before
> Christ the royal Master
> Leads against the foe;
> Forward into battle,
> See, his banner go:
>
> Onward Christian soldiers,
> Marching as to war,
> With the cross of Jesus
> Going on before.
> At the sign of triumph
> Satan's legions flee:
> On then Christian soldiers,
> On to victory.

1 **a** Above is an extract from a hymn. What is a hymn?
  b For which Christian denomination would this hymn be appropriate?
  c Why do you think that this hymn would be appropriate for the denomination you have chosen?
2 Why do churches sing hymns?
3 Why do churches have choirs?
4 'Silence is a better way to praise God than singing.' Do you agree? Give reasons for your answer, showing that you have thought about more than one point of view.

Task 4

> **The first miracle at Cana** (John 2:1–11)
>
> On the third day a wedding took place at Cana in Galilee. Jesus' mother was there, and his disciples had also been invited to the wedding. When the wine was gone, Jesus' mother said to him, "They have no more wine." "Dear woman, why do you involve me?" Jesus replied. "My time has not yet come." His mother said to the servants, "Do whatever he tells you." Nearby stood six stone water jars, the kind used by the Jews for ceremonial washing, each holding from twenty to thirty gallons. Jesus said to the servants, "Fill the jars with water"; so they filled them to the brim. Then he told them, "Now draw some out and take it to the master of the banquet." They did so, and the master of the banquet tasted the water that had been turned into wine. He did not realize where it had come from, though the servants who had drawn the water knew. Then he called the bridegroom aside and said "Everyone brings out the choice wine first and then the cheaper wine after the guests have had too much to drink; but you have saved the best till now." This, the first of his miraculous signs, Jesus performed at Cana in Galilee. He thus revealed his glory, and his disciples put their faith in him.

1 Why might a passage such as the account of the first miracle at Cana be read in Church?
2 What will the reading in the service be called?
3 Is there any festival or occasion when you think that reading the account of the first miracle at Cana would be particularly appropriate? Give reasons for your answer.

Task 5

'Pentecostal worship will only appeal to young people.' Do you agree? Give reasons for your answer, showing that you have thought about more than one point of view.

Topic 1 Roman Catholic and Anglican churches

What is ...?

Adoration is to show honour and worship to God.

The form of worship that takes place in a Christian denomination shapes the design of the building in which the people of that denomination worship. The reasons why Christian places of worship are built include:

- to provide a place for people to worship together
- it is believed by some Christians that building a beautiful place of worship is an act of worship in itself because it shows adoration of God.

What do you think?

'God would prefer people to feed the hungry people of the world rather than spend money building beautiful places of worship.' Do you agree? Give reasons for your answer, showing that you have thought about more than one point of view.

Some churches have **spires**. A spire is a symbolic 'finger' pointing the way to heaven. Christians see spires as a reminder to people that it is through the worship of God in the Christian faith that the way is opened for them to God and heaven.

Some churches have a spire

Many churches have a **belfry**. This is the place in which the bells hang and are rung to call people to worship. Peals of bells are rung at weddings to express the joy of the occasion, and a single bell is tolled at funerals to show that it is a solemn time.

Some churches have a belfry

What is...?

An **altar** is a place of sacrifice. In the Christian tradition it is a table made of wood or stone and is used for the Eucharist.

Activity

Look at page 77. What is the Eucharist? How do the Roman Catholic Church and the Church of England celebrate Holy Communion?

The most significant feature in the Roman Catholic Church and the Church of England is the **altar.** The altar is the focal point of the most important service in these two denominations, Holy Communion. Candles are lit on the altar at the beginning of each service as a reminder that Christ, the Light of the World, will be present during the service. The two denominations believe that salvation comes through the bread and wine and therefore central to the service is the consecration of the bread and wine.

Activity

1 Draw the plan of the Church of England parish church in your book.
2 Write down the descriptions of the features in a parish church that are listed in the text below.
3 Beside the description of each feature, write the correct number from the plan that matches it.

The Church of England church

Features in a typical parish church include:

- the **communion rail,** where people kneel to take the bread and wine during Holy Communion
- the **chancel,** which is the area of the church that contains the altar and the choir stalls
- the main body of the church, called the **nave**
- the **lectern,** on which the Bible is placed. The Bible is read from this stand during the services
- the **choir stalls,** where the choir sit
- the **font,** which contains the water for baptism
- the **sanctuary,** which contains the altar and is the holiest part of the church
- a raised platform called a **pulpit,** where the vicar (priest) stands to preach the sermon
- **pews,** in which the congregation sit during the service.
- an **altar,** which is a table made of wood or stone that is used for the Eucharist

A plan of a typical parish church in the Church of England

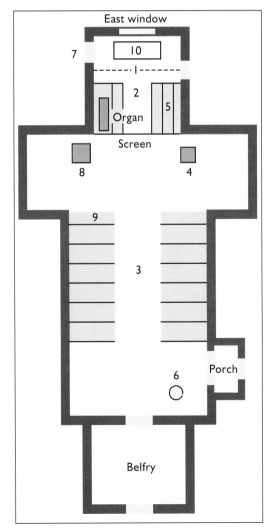

7: Christian places of worship

What is...?

A **confessional** is an enclosed stall in a Roman Catholic church in which a priest hears people's confession.

Activity

Look at page 8. What is the role of a priest in confession?

In a Roman Catholic church there will be confessionals

The Roman Catholic church

The design of a Roman Catholic church is very similar to that of the Church of England, but in addition there are confessionals.

Many churches in the Church of England will also have side chapels. In Roman Catholic churches there is always at least one side chapel, which will be dedicated to the Virgin Mary. There may also be statues of Jesus and saints. People will say prayers to the person represented by the statue asking them to speak to God on their behalf. After prayers have been said people will often light candles in front of the statue. This is a way of honouring and saying thank you to the person in the statue.

Questions

1 Explain **two** reasons why churches are built.
2 Why do some churches have spires?
3 What is a belfry used for?
4 **a** What is the most important feature of churches in the Roman Catholic and Church of England tradition?
   b Why is this the most important feature of these churches?
5 Where will the priest stand to give the sermon in these churches?
6 There will always be a Lady Chapel in a Roman Catholic church. To whom is this chapel dedicated?
7 What are the confessionals in a Roman Catholic church used for?
8 Why might people light candles in front of the statues in the church?

The Eastern Orthodox church

The **dome** is above the nave and represents heaven. The dome reminds people that to gain God's blessing it is necessary to accept salvation through Christ. It is circular to represent the eternity of God. Very often there is a picture of God painted in the middle of its ceiling.

The **nave** is the area below the dome. The congregation stand in the nave throughout the service as the only seats are for the old and sick, at the side of the church. People move around freely during the services. They may pray before icons and light candles. The nave represents the world in which people live, and which is beneath heaven. Orthodox Christians believe the world is sinful and only Christ and the Holy Spirit can lead them out of the darkness of sin.

The **iconostasis** is a screen painted with pictures that are called icons. These include pictures of Christ, the Virgin Mary, John the Baptist and the disciples. Above the screen is a crucifix, to remind people of how Jesus rescued the world and opened the way back to God. The screen divides the nave from the **sanctuary**, which represents heaven. The screen is a reminder that heaven is hidden from the world's view. In the sanctuary, the area behind the screen is the **Holy Throne** (altar), on which Christ is believed to be present during the service of Holy Communion (Divine Liturgy). In the centre of the screen are the **Royal Doors,** which are opened and closed during the Divine Liturgy. These represent the link between heaven and earth brought by Jesus. When open the congregation is reminded that through Christ, God has opened a new way for man to be united with God despite the barrier of sin. It is through Christ that the worshipper receives a glimpse of heaven. Through these doors, the priests carry the Gospels and the communion elements during the Divine Liturgy.

The exterior of an Eastern Orthodox church

The nave is the area below the dome

An iconostasis in an Orthodox church

Questions

1 What do the following features of the Orthodox church represent?
   i the dome
   ii the nave
   iii the sanctuary
   iv the iconostasis
   v the Royal Doors
   vi the Holy Throne.
2 How is the design of an Orthodox church influenced by Orthodox beliefs?

Topic 2 Free churches

Activity

Look at pages 96 to 97. List the major differences between the various forms of worship in the Free churches.

There are several designs of church buildings in the Free Church tradition. This is because of the many different styles of worship in the Protestant tradition. The emphasis in the design of these churches will be on the Word of God, as these denominations believe that it is through listening to God's Word that people learn how to live as God wishes and to achieve salvation.

The focal point in Methodist and Baptist churches will be the pulpit

The design of Methodist and Baptist churches is very similar. The focal point in both churches is the pulpit, because these churches believe that the most important part of any service is listening to the word of God. There will not be an altar, as these churches do not believe that Christ's sacrifice is repeated during the service of Holy Communion. There will be a communion table, because these denominations believe that the service of Holy Communion is only a memorial to strengthen faith and fellowship.

The Methodist church will have a bowl to act as a font for infant baptism. The bowl is placed on the communion table during baptisms. In a Baptist church there will be a pool, because this denomination baptises adults by total immersion.

Questions

1 **a** What is the main feature of Methodist and Baptist churches?
  b Why is this the main feature in these churches?
2 An altar is not used in the Methodist and Baptist churches. Where is Holy Communion performed instead?
3 **a** What is the major difference between a Methodist and a Baptist church?
  b Why is there this difference between the church design of the two denominations?

The **Salvation Army** and the **Society of Friends** (Quakers) do not hold services of Holy Communion and baptism so they do not need to include an altar, communion table, font or baptistry in the design of their places of worship.

 ## *What do you think?*

A **citadel** is a fortress on high ground. Why do you think that the Salvation Army have chosen to call their place of worship a citadel?

Activity

Look at page 86. Design a place of worship in which Pentecostal Christians can worship.

A **citadel** is the building in which the Salvation Army worship. The most important part of the citadel is the **Worship Hall**. The hall is simply furnished, with rows of chairs facing a platform on which the officers, choir and Army band sit. At the front of the platform is a reading desk from which the worship is led. Also at the front of the platform is the **Holiness table** on which there is a large, open Bible, as a sign that Christians draw nearer to God through his message. Behind the table is the **Mercy seat**. This is a plain wooden bench on which people who have sinned are invited to sit and pray for forgiveness or to make a public commitment of their faith. At the back of the platform will be the banners used in the Salvation Army parades.

Inside a Salvation Army citadel

A **Friend's Meeting House** is the place in which members of the Society of Friends (Quakers) meet together. The Quakers sit in a circle and there is often a low table in the centre on which there is a Bible, 'Quaker Faith and Practice' (a guide to their beliefs), and some flowers. Often there are no pictures or statues in the Meeting House because Quakers prefer everything to be plain and simple.

As many Christians use their place of worship for both worship and other activities, there is often an additional area that can be used for community activities. These may include:

- Sunday school for the children
- coffee or a community meal after the services
- Bible classes
- social events
- fundraising activities such as jumble sales
- scouts, guides, play groups and other similar activities for young people.

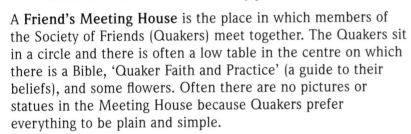 ## *Questions*

1 Describe the Worship Hall used for worship by members of the Salvation Army.
2 How is the design of a Friends' Meeting House influenced by the Quaker style of worship?
3 'A church should only be used for public worship.' Do you agree? Give reasons for your answer, showing that you have thought about more than one point of view.

Do you understand...
Christian places of worship?

Task 1

1 Why do Christians build places of worship?
2 What influences the design of a place of Christian worship?
3 Design a suitable place of worship for use by members of the Roman Catholic Church.
4 Explain the reasons for the features you have included in your design.

The interior of a Church of England parish church

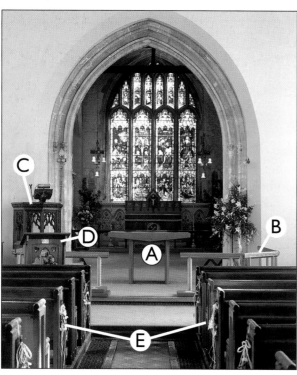

Task 2

1 a Look at the picture of the interior of a Church of England parish church. Name each of the features marked A to E in the picture.
  b Explain what each feature is used for in the Church of England.
2 a State **two** ways in which this interior would differ from the interior of a Roman Catholic church.
  b Give reasons for each of these differences.
3 a State **two** other ways in which this interior would differ from the interior of a Salvation Army citadel.
  b Give the reasons for each of these differences.
4 Do you think that it matters what church buildings look like inside? Give reasons for your answer, showing that you have thought about more than one point of view.

Task 3

1 Describe in detail an Orthodox church. Explain how the design of the church is important for the style of worship which takes place there.
2 Describe and explain **two** differences between the Orthodox church you have described and a Roman Catholic church.
3 'It is wrong to appeal for money to repair churches.' Do you agree? Give reasons for your answer, showing that you have thought about more than one point of view.

Task 4

1 a Describe a pulpit.
   a What is a pulpit used for?
2 a What is an altar?
   b What is an altar used for?
   c Why is a pulpit rather than an altar the
      most important feature in a Methodist
      church?
3 State and explain **one** major difference
   between a Methodist and a Baptist church.

A pulpit

Task 5

1 What name is given to the building in which
   the Salvation Army meet for worship?
2 Describe in detail a Salvation Army place of
   worship. Explain how the design of the
   building is important for the style of worship
   that takes place there.

People praying at the Mercy
seat in a Holiness meeting

Task 6

1 Quakers feel that the simplicity of a Friends'
   Meeting House gives a better communal sense
   of worship. Do you think a simple place of
   worship or an ornate building would give a
   better sense of communal worship? Give
   reasons for your opinion and include
   references to different Christian
   denominations' points of view.

Task 7

1 Why do Christians meet together for other
   activities besides worship?
2 What sort of activities might take place on the
   church site besides worship?
3 Suggest some activities that might be suitable
   for a church youth club. Explain the reason(s)
   for each choice.
4 'It is the responsibility of the
   local churches to stop young
   people getting bored.' Do you
   agree? Give reasons for your
   answer, showing that you have
   thought about more than one
   point of view.

Worship in a Friends' Meeting House

† **ST CUTHBERT'S PARISH CHURCH** †

TIMES OF WORSHIP		BROWNIES AND GUIDES	
		EVERY MONDAY	6.30 – 7.30 PM
SUNDAY EUCHARIST	8.30 AM		
FAMILY SERVICE	11.00 AM	BIBLE-STUDY CLASSES	
		WEDNESDAY	7.30 – 8.30 PM
SUNDAY SCHOOL	11.00 AM		
EVENSONG	6.30 PM	CHOIR PRACTICE	
		FRIDAY	8.00 – 9.00 PM
		YOUTH CLUB	
EVERY WEDNESDAY		TUESDAYS AND THURSDAYS	
SERVICE OF		IN THE CHURCH HALL	
HOLY COMMUNION	8.30 AM		6.30 – 7.30 PM

A church noticeboard

Topic 1 — Types of prayer

What is...?

Meditation is to focus the mind on a specific subject.

Prayer is both talking and listening to God.

Christians use prayer in both public and private worship as a way of communicating with God. Christians believe prayer is not only talking to God but also listening to what guidance God may give them. Prayers take many forms. They may include extracts from the Bible or have been written by other people or made up for the specific occasion by the person praying. The prayers may be said in silence or aloud. Many Christians use **meditation** in prayer to concentrate on the voice of God and Jesus in an attempt to come closer to them. They try to close their mind to everyday things so that they can hear the inner voice of God. There are different methods of meditation, which may involve concentrating on some aspect of the life of Jesus, repeating his name or reciting a short prayer.

There are four major types of prayer:

- **adoration** prayers are prayers in praise of God
- **confession** prayers are prayers in which people admit to God that they have committed sins
- **thanksgiving** prayers are prayers that thank God for things He has done or provided
- **supplication** prayers are prayers that ask God for something.

Activity

1. Write down each type of prayer in your book.
2. Make up an example of each type of prayer.
3. **Grace** refers to prayers said to thank God for his gifts. Grace is often said before or after meals to thank God for the gift of food. The most famous grace is 'For what we are about to receive may the Lord make us truly thankful'. Write your own grace that could be used before a meal.

What do you think?

When Christians finish praying they will say '**Amen**'. Amen means 'so let it be'. Why do you think Christians say 'so let it be' at the end of their prayers?

Activity

Look at page 86. What is a Charismatic Christian?

People take up a variety of positions when they pray. Some may stand while others kneel. Some positions are preferred by particular Christian denominations. Charismatic Christians often raise their hands as they pray. Quakers remain seated, Roman Catholics kneel and Orthodox Christians stand.

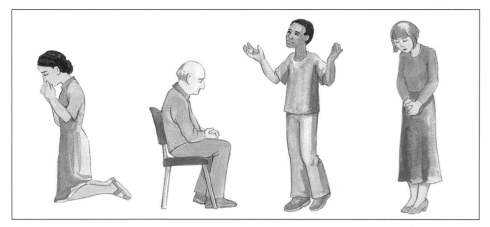

Christians adopt different positions for prayer

What do you think?

What do you think the different positions of prayer are trying to achieve, or to show about the individual Christian's relationship to God?

Jesus taught that prayers should be said in his name as he had won access to God through his suffering and death on the cross. Many Christians end their prayers, 'through Jesus Christ, Our Lord', to show that they remember that it is through Jesus that they are able to speak to God. Jesus taught that people must be persistent in prayer and not expect answers straight away. Jesus taught that Christians must pray with humility and true faith. In the Gospels, there are several occasions when Jesus prayed. Jesus prayed because:

- Jesus had a close personal relationship with God since he was God's son. Prayer was the means by which he could talk to his father, God.
- Jesus believed that God created everything and that God has a purpose for His creation. Prayer is the means by which this purpose can be discovered.
- Jesus had to face situations in which he needed support. Prayer was the means by which God's wisdom, power and strength could come to him.

Christians have followed the example of Jesus in their use of prayer, and use prayers to speak to God, listen to God and to receive guidance, support and comfort from God.

Questions

1 What is prayer?
2 What is meditation?
3 State and explain the **four** types of prayer.
4 What does 'amen' mean?
5 Why do many prayers end with 'through Jesus Christ our Lord'?
6 Why did Jesus pray?
7 'It does not matter how you pray so long as you pray.' Do you agree? Give reasons for your answer, showing that you have thought about more than one point of view.

Topic 2 — The Lord's Prayer

 Activity

Look at page 28. What is a sermon?

When he was standing on a hillside, Jesus explained to his followers how they were to behave as God would wish. The talk has become known as the **Sermon on the Mount**, and is found in the Gospel of Matthew, chapters 5, 6 and 7.

During the talk Jesus taught his followers how to pray and he gave them an example of a suitable prayer. Christians call the prayer the **Lord's Prayer**, because it was taught by the Lord, Jesus Christ. It is also known as the **Pattern Prayer** as it provides a pattern for Christians to follow in prayer, to ensure that they pray in the way God and Jesus would want.

Jesus gave his followers a prayer to use during the Sermon on the Mount

The Lord's Prayer

Our Father which art in heaven,

Hallowed be thy name.

Thy kingdom come.

Thy will be done on earth as it is in heaven.

Give us this day our daily bread;

And forgive us our trespasses

As we forgive those who trespass against us.

And lead us not into temptation, but deliver us from evil.

The doxology

Christians have added an extra line to the Lord's Prayer to thank and praise God. This is called the doxology and it says,
'For Thine is the Kingdom, the power and the glory, For ever and ever. Amen'

The meaning of the Lord's Prayer

'**Our Father which art in heaven, hallowed be thy name**' This line is praising God (adoration). It is reminding people that God is in heaven and yet is close to people. God is like a father who loves his children. God's name is sacred and holy and must be treated with respect. The third commandment 'You must not take God's name in vain' must not be broken.

'**Thy kingdom come. Thy will be done on earth as it is in heaven**' This line in the Lord's Prayer is asking God to establish his rule on earth and to make people obedient to Him. This line is a form of supplication. If God's kingdom was established on earth, Christians believe the world would be like heaven, where everything happens as God wishes, and there would be no sin in the world.

'**Give us this day our daily bread**' continues the request for all that is needed to establish God's kingdom on earth. In the Bible 'bread' stands for strength. Christians believe that people need not only physical strength from food and drink but also spiritual strength from the Word of God to overcome temptation.

'**And forgive us our trespasses, as we forgive those who trespass against us**' This part of the Lord's Prayer is a confession. Christians are admitting that they commit sins and are asking for God's forgiveness. Unless Christians forgive others then they believe that they cannot be forgiven either by God or by other people. Forgiveness is something that has to be accepted as well as given.

'**And lead us not into temptation but deliver us from evil**' is another supplication as it is asking for God's help not to give in to the desire to do something which would be against God's laws. This would be a sin. There is also a request for God's protection from all the disasters that could happen in life.

A **doxology** is a liturgical sentence praising God, ie the words used in the sentence have been set down by the Church.

Write out the Lord's Prayer in your book and learn it.

Look at page 13. What Christian understanding of God is found in the Apostles' Creed?

Questions

1 Why is the Lord's Prayer called the Lord's Prayer?
2 Why is the Lord's Prayer also known as the Pattern Prayer?
3 **a** What ending is added to the Lord's Prayer?
   b Why do you think that Christians have added this ending?
4 In your own words, explain what Christians mean when they say the words of the Lord's Prayer.
5 'The Lord's Prayer is outdated.' Do you agree? Give reasons for your answer, showing that you have thought about more than one point of view.

Topic 3 — Aids to prayer

Activity

Look at page 100. What is meditation?

Meditation

Christians use **meditation** to help them to concentrate on God. Sometimes Christians will withdraw from everyday life to give their full attention to God and Jesus. This is called 'going on retreat'. People may go to a monastery or a convent for a period of retreat. Other Christians may use a specific prayer or an object to help them concentrate while they are praying.

Some Christians may go on retreat to the island of Iona

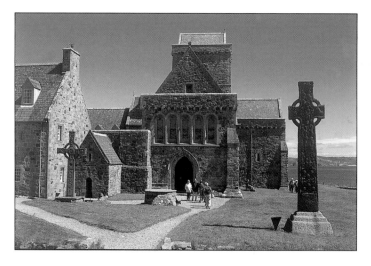

Many Christians use the Bible in private worship

The Bible

Christians use the **Bible** as an aid to private worship. Individuals set aside a quiet time each day for Bible-reading and prayer. Christians often use a set of Bible-notes to help them understand the passages they are reading and to give them an order of Bible-readings to follow. Christians believe that by reading passages from the Bible, an individual can find solutions to personal problems, better understanding of the teachings of Christianity and spiritual strength.

Crucifixes and crosses

Other Christians use either a **crucifix** or a **cross** as an aid to prayer and meditation.

A crucifix contains the body of Christ nailed to the cross. It is used to remind people of the suffering of Jesus on the cross to gain forgiveness from God for the sins of the world.

An empty cross reminds Christians that through his sacrifice, Jesus conquered sin and death. Christians hope that by following Jesus they will achieve eternal life with God after death. An empty cross helps Christians concentrate on what may be the rewards of following Jesus and being obedient to God.

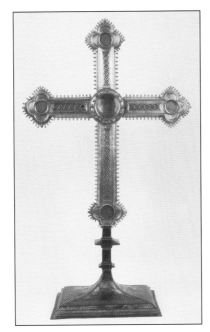

An empty cross

A crucifix

Statues

Some Christians use statues to help them concentrate on their prayers. The statue may be of Jesus, the Virgin Mary or saints. As they pray, Christians think about the life of the person depicted and how they could follow the example set by this person in their own life. Christians may ask the person to speak to God on their behalf.

 **What is ...?**

> An **icon** is a devotional painting or carving, usually on wood, of Christ, the Virgin Mary or another holy figure such as a saint.

A statue of the Virgin Mary

Icons

In the **Orthodox Church**, pictures called icons are used as an aid to prayer. These holy pictures are painted according to strict rules and are regarded as a 'window to heaven'. People pray to statues and icons of the Virgin Mary and saints to speak to God on their behalf. This is called an **intercession**.

An icon of Jesus

Activity

> Look at page 94. Why are candles often lit in front of statues after prayers have been said in front of them?

What is ...?

A **rosary** is a string of beads used to help keep count of prayers.

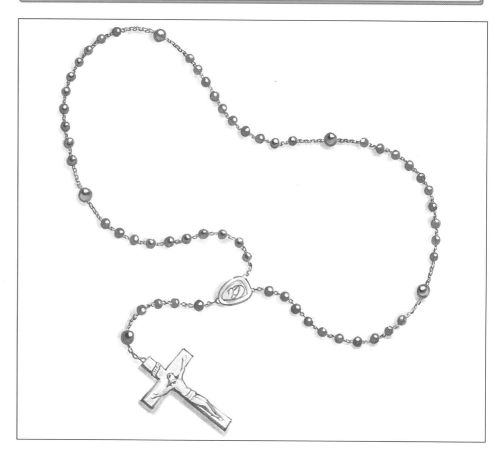

A rosary

The rosary

In the **Roman Catholic Church,** the rosary is used to help Christians concentrate on their prayers. The prayers begin at the crucifix and continue round a circle of small beads divided into five groups of ten beads. Each group of ten beads is called a **decade.** In between each decade is a larger bead. There are fifteen decades in the complete rosary but the beads only cover five of them. When a Roman Catholic prays the rosary, they choose to concentrate on one of three subjects related to the life of Jesus. These three subjects, or mysteries, are:

- the Joyful Mysteries, which are linked to events associated with the birth of Jesus
- the Sorrowful Mysteries, which are linked to events associated with the death of Jesus
- the Glorious Mysteries, which are linked to events associated with the resurrection of Jesus.

A Roman Catholic will run the beads through his or her fingers and say the set prayers at each bead while concentrating on the Mysteries chosen.

The 'Gloria' is said on the large beads to end each decade:

'Glory be to the Father, and to the Son, and to the Holy Spirit, as it was in the beginning, is now, and ever shall be, world without end, Amen.'

The 'Our Father' prayer is then said, to start the next decade.

The 'Our Father' prayer is said here

One 'Hail Mary' is said on each small bead:

'Hail Mary, full of Grace, the Lord is with thee. Blessed art thou among women and blessed is the fruit of thy womb, Jesus.

Holy Mary, Mother of God, pray for us sinners, now and at the hour of our death, Amen.'

The 'Gloria' is said on this bead.

One 'Hail Mary' is said on each of these three beads.

The 'Apostles' Creed' is said on this bead.

Prayers are said at each bead of the rosary

Draw and label the rosary in your book.

Questions

1 Why do Christians use the Bible as an aid to prayer?
2 Describe and explain **two** other aids to prayer used by Christians.
3 **a** Which denomination uses the rosary?
   b Explain how the rosary is used to aid prayer.
4 'A Christian should be able to pray without any need of anything to help them pray.' Do you agree? Give reasons for your answer, showing that you have thought about more than one point of view.

Topic 4: Pilgrimage

A **pilgrimage** is a journey undertaken for a special reason, or to a special place, usually a holy place.

Pilgrims on a Palm Sunday procession down from the Mount of Olives in Jerusalem

Many Christians undertake a **pilgrimage** as a way of worshipping God. It is not compulsory for Christians to make a pilgrimage but many Christians do make a journey to places associated with Jesus or a saint. They hope to receive some spiritual blessing or healing at the place visited. Many Christians say that they feel a sense of spiritual renewal after undertaking a pilgrimage. The reasons for making a pilgrimage include:

- to be healed
- to ask for something
- to give thanks for something
- to say sorry to God for sins committed
- to achieve eternal life
- to deepen faith
- to show devotion to Jesus or a particular saint.

Activity

Look at page 49. What are the Stations of the Cross?

Many Christians will go to the Holy Land to visit the places associated with the events in the life of Jesus, especially Bethlehem and Jerusalem. A popular time to visit Jerusalem for Christians is Good Friday so that they can follow the actual Stations of the Cross at the place where the events took place.

The sick are brought on pilgrimage to Lourdes in the hopes of a miraculous cure

Another popular place of pilgrimage for Christians, especially Roman Catholics, is Lourdes in France. The place is associated with Saint Bernadette, a peasant girl, who had visions of the Virgin Mary in 1858, when she was 14 years old. Saint Bernadette claimed that the Virgin Mary told her that water in a spring in the hills near Lourdes had healing powers and that a chapel was to be built at the site. Since 1873, millions of pilgrims have journeyed to Lourdes. Some have claimed to be healed by the water and others that they have returned home with a sense of peace.

8: Prayer and private worship

Look at page 35.

What do you think?

If the water of Lourdes does not have miraculous healing powers, what other reasons could explain the many accounts of healing associated with Lourdes?

Activity

Look at page 35. What is the Annunciation?

In England, Walsingham in Norfolk is a place of pilgrimage for Christians. It is popular as a place of pilgrimage for members of both the Church of England and the Roman Catholic Church. A shrine to the Virgin Mary was built in Walsingham in the eleventh century after Richeldis of Faversham was told in a vision to build a replica of the house in Nazareth where the **Annunciation** took place. There is a well at the site which is believed to have similar healing properties to the water at Lourdes.

Many Christians walk to the shrine during Holy Week to share Jesus' journey to the cross. On the journey to the shrine they think of all that Jesus achieved for the world by his suffering and sacrifice.

The restored image of Our Lady of Walsingham holding the infant Jesus

Activity

1 Choose **one** of the following places of Christian pilgrimage:
   Assissi, in Italy
   Canterbury, in England
   Fatima, in Portugal
   Knock, in Ireland
   Medjugorje, in the former Yugoslavia
   Vatican City, Rome, in Italy.
2 Find out as much as you can about pilgrimage to the place chosen.
3 Explain in your book why the place chosen is a popular place of pilgrimage.

What do you think?

'Pilgrimage is no more than an excuse for a holiday.' Do you agree? Give reasons for your opinion, showing that you have thought about more than one point of view.

Questions

1 What is a pilgrimage?
2 Explain **three** reasons why a Christian might choose to go on pilgrimage.
3 Why did Lourdes become a place of pilgrimage?
4 'Miracles don't happen.' Do you agree? Give reasons for your answer, showing that you have thought about more than one point of view.

Do you understand...

Christian prayer and private worship?

Task 1

1 What do Christians mean when they speak of prayer and private worship?
2 Why do many Christians use meditation as part of their private worship?
3 What is a grace and when might one be said?
4 Why do Christians end their prayers with 'amen'?
5 Why do many Christians add that the prayer is 'through Jesus Christ, Our Lord'?
6 'It is important to set time aside each day for prayer.' Do you agree? Give reasons for your answer, showing that you have thought about more than one point of view.

Task 2

A *Dear God we live in a beautiful world in which you have provided us with everything we need. We thank you for all your gifts. Amen.*

Dear God help us to think of others rather than ourselves. Help us to be less selfish and to be more willing to share what we have with those people who have nothing. Help us to remember the starving people of the world and to work to overcome their problems. Amen B

C *Dear God I know that I do not always behave as you would want. I am often angry with others. I see the faults in others but I do not always see my own faults. I am sorry for all the things that I have done against your will. Amen*

Dear God, You are the Almighty Father, creator of everything who deserves our love, praise and obedience. We seek to serve you in every thing we do. Amen. D

People pray for different reasons

1 Explain the **four** main types of prayer.
2 State the type of prayer each of the people labelled A to D in the picture is using, and explain your choice.
3 a What position of prayer might be appropriate for each prayer A to D?
   b Explain why you think each of these positions seems appropriate.
4 'Saying what you feel rather than using a made-up prayer is the best way to pray.' Do you agree? Give reasons for your answer, showing that you have thought about more than one point of view.

Task 3

'Lord Jesus Christ, Son of God, have mercy on me, a sinner.'
This prayer is known as the Jesus prayer. It is repeated many times during prayer as a way of helping people meditate on Jesus and the need to follow Jesus if salvation is to be achieved.

1 Why do Christians meditate?

2 Why might they use the Jesus prayer in meditation?

3 Do you think set prayers like the Jesus prayer are helpful to Christians? Give reasons for your answer.

Task 4

1 What was the Sermon on the Mount?

2 Why do you think Jesus gave his followers a prayer to use?

3 What is the prayer given by Jesus called?

4 In your own words, explain what Christians mean when they say 'Our Father which art in heaven, hallowed be thy name'.

5 In your own words, explain what Christians are asking for when they say 'Give us this day our daily bread' and 'Forgive us our trespasses' in the Lord's Prayer.

6 Do you think a person who does not use the Lord's Prayer can claim to be a real Christian? Give reasons for your answer, showing that you have thought about more than one point of view.

Task 5

1 Explain how a Christian might use the Bible in private worship.

2 Why would a Christian want to use the Bible as part of their worship?

3 'You cannot worship on your own.' Do you agree? Give reasons for your answer, showing that you have thought about more than one point of view.

The Virgin Mary with the Infant Jesus

Task 6

1 What is the picture opposite called?

2 Which Christian denomination uses this type of picture as an aid to prayer?

3 Explain how these pictures are used as an aid to private worship.

4 'A picture is a picture not an aid to prayer.' Do you agree? Give reasons for your answer, showing that you have thought about more than one point of view.

Task 7

1 What is a rosary?

2 In which denomination is a rosary used?

3 Why do Christians in this denomination use a rosary?

4 Explain how the rosary is used in prayer.

Task 8

1 a Name **three** places to which Christians might go on pilgrimage.

 b Explain why each of these sites is important and briefly what pilgrims may do there.

2 Explain the ways in which visiting these sites may be important for a Christian's spiritual life.

3 'God is everywhere so there is no need to go on pilgrimage to find Him.' Do you agree? Give reasons for your answer showing that you have thought about more than one point of view.

A Christian praying with the rosary

Revision

Careful revision brings success

Revision timetable

Work out how many weeks are left before your 'mock' examination or the GCSE examinations start. Make a plan of all the topics you need to revise and all the leisure activities you wish to continue during the revision period. Fill in study periods and leisure periods. At the beginning of each week decide which topics you are going to study during that week. **Do not leave revision to the last minute.**

Make the best use of revision time

- You need a suitable environment in which to revise. Some people need to revise in total silence, whereas other people like music in the background. Use whichever method helps your revision.
- You need to get down to work according to the timetable **you** have drawn up. Revise the topic you have written down, and do not waste time deciding what you are going to do.

Revision techniques

Successful revision involves active learning. There are a variety of revision techniques which can help you to understand and memorise information. You need to find which technique is best for you.

Note-taking
- Summaries of the information can help you remember the information. As you study each section of your notes, write down the important points.
- Learn these points and then cover up the notes and rewrite them from memory.
- Check off your list from memory against your original list, and note any points you got wrong or forgot to include.

Practise past questions
- Use past questions you have worked through in class, or questions from past examination papers, to help you understand the work.
- Answer the questions, in note form, using your notes.
- Cover up your answer and work through the question again without notes.
- Check off your answer from memory against your original list, and note any points you got wrong or forgot to include.

Use the 'Do you understand' sections of this book
Work through each set of tasks in each of the sections in this book to help you to develop your skills and understanding.